DARKNESS WAS THEIR ONLY HOPE OF SECRECY

A gentle surf washed Atcheson and Foley up onto the rocky beach and they carefully crawled a few feet away from the water. They lay motionless for a few minutes listening and watching for any sound or sight of the enemy. Then they carefully uncovered their waterproofed pistols and several grenades and moved cautiously across the rough pebble beach. They came to a steep, sloping embankment made from large stones and paused to listen again.

As they started to climb the wall they noticed that the moon was rising. Once on top of the embankment, they made their way quickly to the bridge at the mouth of the tunnel. They could see no enemy pillboxes or gun emplacements and everything seemed perfect, except for one thing: the moon.

When they turned and looked back to the beach they became alarmed—they could clearly see their rubber boat some 200 yards offshore, the landing craft another 500 yards out, and, behind it, nearly three miles away, the *Diachenko*, their mother ship. It was almost a daylight scene.

Then Atcheson heard the enemy.

The Fighting Elite™

U.S. NAVY SEALS

IAN PADDEN

BANTAM BOOKS
TORONTO • NEW YORK • LONDON • SYDNEY • AUCKLAND

To Lynda Cresswell:
the only female "tadpole" I ever knew.

And to "Snoopy,"
who both amused and tormented us.

THE FIGHTING ELITE™: U.S. NAVY SEALS

A Bantam Book / June 1985

Produced by Bruck Communications, Inc.
157 West 57th Street, New York, NY 10019.

Cover photo courtesy U.S. Navy

Inside photos courtesy D.A.V.A.

ISBN 0-553-24954-1

Published simultaneously in the United States and Canada

Bantam Books are published by Bantam Books, Inc. Its trade-
mark, consisting of the words "Bantam Books" and the por-
trayal of a rooster, is Registered in U.S. Patent and Trademark
Office and in other countries. Marca Registrada. Bantam
Books, Inc., 666 Fifth Avenue, New York, New York 10103.

PRINTED IN THE UNITED STATES OF AMERICA

H   0 9 8 7 6 5 4 3 2 1

ACKNOWLEDGMENTS

Many thanks to Lieutenant Commander Donald C. Lewis USN, Public Affairs Office, NAS Point Mugu, for invaluable assistance; Dr. Vincent A. Transano, Historical Information Branch, Naval Facilities Engineering Command; and to the Defense Audio Visual Aid Department, Washington, D.C.

Special thanks must go to several long-standing friends who helped to ensure that I did not allude to anything that might compromise our national security.

IAN PADDEN

CONTENTS

1

BATTLEFIELD LOG:
Morocco, North Africa—November, 1942

It was almost 0330 hours on the morning of November 8, 1942, as the open-decked, Higgens-type assault boat approached the mouth of the Wadi Sebou River on the west coast of French Morocco.

Huddled down inside the boat were seventeen men of the United States Navy, led by Lieutenant Mark Starkweather, and stacked around them was an array of explosive charges and wire-cutting equipment. They were about to become the first Allied personnel to receive close quarter enemy fire in Operation Torch, the first great Allied amphibious assault landing.

Operation Torch had three task forces and three different areas of operation on the North African coast. The Eastern Task Force was to land near the port of Algiers, the Central Task Force was to land near the city of Oran, and the Western Task Force was to land at the mouth of the Wadi Sebou River near the city of Casablanca. The principle targets were the cities named; but instead of being taken in a direct attack, they were to be taken in a flanking move by troops landing farther along the coast, who would then swing toward the cities from the landward side.

The Western Task Force, under the command of Major General George S. Patton, comprised elements of the 9th Infantry Division and the 2nd Armored Division. As Patton's men were being transferred from their transport ships into their landing craft, Lieutenant Starkweather's boat was heading through rough seas and rain squalls straight into the river mouth.

Starkweather and most of his men were salvage experts who had helped raise some of the sunken ships from the bottom of Pearl Harbor after the savage Japanese bombing on December 7, 1941. They had been recruited only two months previously for the sole purpose of destroying a massive boom and net arrangement that was strung across the Wadi Sebou River just inside the jetties that flanked the mouth of the river. Immediately behind the boom was the harbor of Port Lyautey, now called Kenitra. The Allied commanders had determined that the boom defense had to be cleared and the port secured as quickly as possible.

It was not actually the port that the Allied commanders were interested in—it was the strategically located airfield behind it. Capturing the airfield before it was destroyed by the enemy was a priority as it would allow Allied troops, heavy support equipment, and fighter aircraft to be flown in quickly to reinforce the main amphibious force when it had cleared the beaches.

Lieutenant Starkweather and his team had been given a high-speed course in cable cutting, demolition, and commando raiding tactics, and had then been flown to Europe to join the Western Task Force. They were officially called the Combat Demolition Unit, and as such, they were the forerunners of the Underwater Demolition Teams and the SEALs.

Reconnaissance photographs and maps showed that

the boom was overlooked by the great stone-built Casbah fortress. The fortress was known to house a variety of artillery pieces, ranging from 75-mm howitzers to the big 155-mm guns of the main coastal battery. There was also an assortment of rapid firing 37-mm guns, mortars, and heavy machine guns.

Intelligence information suggested that the Casbah garrison was manned by the Vichy French and that they would perhaps offer only token resistance. However, it was also known that the German troops reinforcing the Vichy would certainly offer considerably more than resistance—they would put up a fierce fight.

The Atlantic was living up to its reputation for bad weather as the boat carrying the demolition team left its transport ship for the river mouth. A strong wind was blowing, it was raining, and the sea was rough. There was a long rolling ground swell, which had been nurtured by a chain of fierce storms that had been raging for almost a week some two hundred miles out in the Atlantic.

As the heaving and pitching boat neared the outer harbor entrance, it was struck by a very heavy rain squall. A few moments later the craft was caught on top of a thirty-foot-high ground swell that had just started to break. There was tremendous acceleration as the breaking wave snatched at the boat, striking terror into the hearts of all its occupants, and carried it like a surfboard straight between the jetties on either side of the river mouth.

The coxswain fought to keep the boat straight and applied full power to the already speeding craft to avoid the possibility of being pooped. As the craft raced crazily between the jetties, a red flare was fired by the enemy, who must have been somewhat surprised to see the strange looking object being hurled from the top of a wave through the outer harbor entrance. The coxswain won the fight with the wall of water, and, as the wave spent its energy in a low, spiraling wash, the craft reached the calmer waters inside the river mouth.

With the boat under complete control again, the coxswain steered it slowly along the southern side of the river mouth in the direction of the boom. Starkweather had just begun to think that the enemy had not really seen them when the shooting started. The first fire came from the heavy machine guns and, although it was in the general direction of the Higgens boat, it was somewhat erratic.

However, within a few moments searchlights were fired up from the high walls of the Casbah and almost immediately swept in the direction of the boat. Within seconds the craft was illuminated and the coxswain went into full power. As he worked the boat in a frantic zigzag pattern in an attempt to lose the lights, the 75-mm howitzers joined the machine guns, and huge plumes of spray started to erupt around the boat.

One of the covering destroyers outside the river mouth went into action against the lights on the Casbah, and the enemy immediately responded with its main coastal batteries.

The men in the zigzagging boat were hanging on just as grimly as they had when they were caught on the breaking wave, but the valiant efforts of the coxswain were to no avail; he could not lose the searchlights.

As the element of surprise had now gone completely, Lieutenant Starkweather gave the order to get out of the harbor, and the coxswain swung the boat toward the mouth of the river. Remarkably, neither the boat nor anyone on board had been hit by enemy fire, and at first, the men were only too happy to be heading for the safety of the open sea. Their happiness ended as the craft met the fierce Atlantic surf at the mouth of the river—one form of terror was simply replaced by another.

4

The boat thrashed its way through the surf in violent pitching and twisting movements; men lost their grip and were hurled savagely around the craft. Lieutenant Starkweather was thrown head first into the cockpit coaming and injured his face. One of the sailors had both his ankles broken when he was flung across the equipment in the bottom of the boat, and most of the remaining men suffered minor cuts and bruises.

Once away from the river mouth, the boat returned to the relative calm of the heavy rolling ground swell, and no further injuries were sustained during the journey back to the transport ship.

As the boat reached the transport ship, the main amphibious assault was in progress on the beaches some distance from the river mouth. The assault troops, in their very first experience of an amphibious landing under fire, had to suffer the same heavy, crashing surf that Starkweather's men had endured. It put most of them on the beaches and in front of the enemy more quickly and more violently than they had desired, but intelligence reports later showed that it had surprised the enemy too.

Sea conditions were obviously not favorable for the assault—but it could not be stopped. It took almost two days to get the majority of the troops and their support equipment ashore through the raging Atlantic surf. From the beach they fought their way inland for nearly three miles, and their attempts to get to the Port Lyautey airfield were foiled by the enemy and the Wadi Sebou River. The river was an excellent natural obstacle as it swung in a large protective loop around the airstrip, and its banks were easily defended by the enemy.

The only troops that had not been put ashore were those on the destroyer *Texas,* as they had been assigned the task of taking the airfield when the demolition team had cleared the harbor boom defense.

Patton made it quite clear—he wanted the airfield under his control, and he insisted that these soldiers, specially trained assault troops, remain on board the *Texas* until Starkweather's men could make another attempt. He was convinced that the enemy protecting the harbor entrance would not be as vigilant now that the main assault troops were ashore.

Patton gave the order for another attempt on the night of November 10. He had been hoping that during the delay the heavy seas would subside, but they just became worse; he could wait no longer.

The demolition team boarded their boat a little after midnight on the morning of November 11. With them went a few extra pieces of equipment that they had not carried on their first attempt. They included two light machine guns (supposedly for defense, but perhaps more for comfort in the knowledge that they could at least shoot back), two inflatable rubber boats, and a massive underwater incendiary bomb.

The rubber boats, it was felt, would give them more flexibility and might be useful if the Higgens boat was hit. As for the underwater incendiary bomb, it had been built by one of the team members since their return to the transport ship after the aborted attempt. However, no one was exactly certain what he was going to do with it. There appeared to be all manner of things that could be done with it, but there was no specific use for it, except as a morale-booster. The team took it along with them anyway, just in case.

When the boat broke out from under the lee of the transport ship, everyone realized that the seas were indeed much worse than they had been two nights previously. The waves appeared as veritable mountains on the move intent on only one thing: the destruction of the demolition team and its boat.

The captain of the escort destroyer assigned to give covering fire to the team, should it be needed, was astounded when he learned that the boat was on its way to the river mouth. His escort destroyer was already twisting, rolling, and pitching in the heavy seas and was experiencing great difficulty just remaining on station. If it had to provide covering fire for the demolition team, as it had done on the previous occasion, it was going to be for visual effect only. It would be impossible to hit even the most obvious target with the amount of movement the ship was presently being subjected to.

With the destroyer creaking and groaning, and its crew complaining bitterly at being called to action stations under such conditions, the captain ordered the ship's bow to be swung through the heaving seas in the direction of the river mouth. He had been keeping the destroyer headed into the wind and waves in order to minimize the uncomfortable rolling motion, but such a consideration ceases on all fighting ships when there is work to be done.

In the Higgens boat the demolition team was huddled down behind the gunwales, seeking what little protection was available. The coxswain stood erect in the boat, concentrating his attention on his course and carefully watching the roaring waves for any change of pattern that might further threaten his craft.

As he approached the jetties at the river mouth, the coxswain paid particular attention to the way the giant waves were breaking. The experience of the previous attempt served him well, and he managed to time his approach to catch one of the smaller series of waves. He could see the dark outline of the jetty on the south side of the river mouth; the one to the north was not visible. As the jetty passed within a hundred feet of the boat's starboard side, he, and everyone else on board, waited for the warning flare that would again bring the searchlights and the guns into action. The muffled engines were throttled back as much as possible, without sacrificing control of the vessel, in an attempt to lessen the noise.

The inexperienced might think that throttling back a muffled engine was pointless in the roaring surf, but the coxswain knew better. Mechanical sounds travel great distances over water and can easily be distinguished over the roar of the most deafening waves. There was also the fact that the power settings required to handle the boat in the giant rolling waves off the coast would not be needed when the boat suddenly arrived in the more settled river mouth. It would be pointless to arrive suddenly in the calmer waters with the engines screaming madly, muffled or not.

Lieutenant Starkweather smiled at his second in command, Lieutenant James Darrock, when the flare did not come. A sailor in the bow of the boat acted as lookout and assisted the coxswain with whispered instructions as they moved slowly through the calmer waters close to the south side of the river.

Finding the heavy boom cable with the net suspended below it was not a problem. A line of boats, from which the heavy cable and net were supported, was strung out across the harbor mouth, and it was clearly visible, even in the darkness. Above the cable boom was a smaller wire that was quite taut. It was suspected that this wire might be an alarm device, and the team avoided touching it until the last possible moment.

The team worked quickly on the main cable as they installed a series of explosive charges along a short portion of the boom. The primary cutting device was a heavy explosive cable cutter. During training the device had caused considerable problems as it did not always cut through the practice cables. In the event that it did not work on the Wadi Sebou boom, the team had brought along a large quantity of explosives as backup. As the cable cutter was being installed, so were the backup charges—hundreds of pounds of high explosives. Men were in and out of the water and working feverishly. Everyone expected the dreaded searchlights to come on at any moment and knew that they would be followed immediately by the clattering of the heavy machine guns and the bark of the howitzers.

Two men nervously manned the boat's light machine guns. Starkweather had ordered that their safety catches remain on "safe," and that no shooting was to take place without his direct order while they were working on the cable. The coxswain and the men on the machine guns thought the work on the cable would never finish—waiting under such conditions is always more nerve-racking than working.

With the cutter installed, the men in the water were ordered back into the boat. There was a few moments delay as some final charges were placed on the smaller, taut cable. The cutter charge on the main cable was fired and, to everyone's delight and amazement, it worked on the first attempt. Despite the explosion, there was no immediate response from the enemy; but when the taut cable was sheared, the lights came on and the guns of the Casbah immediately opened fire. As suspected, the smaller cable was an alarm.

The boats supporting the heavy boom cable were being dragged down by the weight of the parted cable, and the current of the river was tugging them downstream. The demolition team had done its job, now all it had to do was get out alive.

One of the boat's machine gunners knocked out two of the big searchlights as the coxswain got the craft underway. The remaining searchlight operators decided that it was safer to turn theirs out, but that did not help the demolition team as mortar flares began to pop up overhead. Fortunately, the wind was blowing strongly again, and the flares were not too much help to the gunners.

It seemed that every conceivable gun in the Casbah was firing on the fast-moving craft. The coxswain took as much evasive action as he could by constantly zigzagging in an erratic manner. Shells started to hit the boat, and the light machine gunners blasted away in the direction of the Casbah. A boat crew's tommy gun joined the shooting, and suddenly every man seemed to have a pistol in his hand and was firing wildly in the direction of the enemy. The Higgens boat was being hit repeatedly now, and Starkweather roared at his men to cease firing in the hope that they would not be such a visible target. This strategy seemed to work somewhat as the enemy fire became less accurate, and the boat received only a few more hits.

As it raced toward the open sea, the boat was starting to take on water, and the coxswain realized that he now had to face the horror of crashing through the giant waves between the jetties. He gave the order to throw as much equipment as possible over the side to lighten the boat. The demolition team did not need to be told twice, they knew what was ahead.

Hundreds of pounds of unused explosives went over the side as the enemy continued to fire on them. Both inflatable boats were quickly heaved over after the explosives, and then came the good luck mascot, the heavy underwater incendiary bomb. Everything that was not immediately usable was heaved overboard, including one of the light machine guns.

As the boat approached the entrance, almost everyone was bailing out water from its bottom; helmets, buckets, boots, and hands were used frantically to lighten the craft. But all bailing had to stop as the men were forced to hang on with all their strength when the first breaking wave crashed over the bow.

The escorting destroyer was in its assigned covering position and started firing in the direction of the Casbah. As the captain had suspected, any form of accuracy was entirely out of the question, but he was quite heartened when he saw some hits in the region of the fortress. He was equally disheartened when all firing from the Casbah stopped; he had no word that the demolition team had succeeded, but he knew for certain that they had been discovered. All that he could do now was to wait until either their boat was spotted by his lookouts or he received official confirmation from the fleet flagship.

In the Higgens boat, men were both elated and frightened. They had succeeded in destroying the boom without anyone being killed or wounded from enemy fire, but they were now in danger of being destroyed by the sea itself.

With some gift of seamanship, the coxswain, his arms aching from the strain of hanging on to the controls and steering the boat, had managed to get through the giant pounding breakers. His only fear now was that the badly holed boat might sink if it came across a giant breaker farther out to sea.

Several of the demolition men were suffering from shock, and others were badly bruised and cut from their work on the boom and the thrashing the boat had taken; but almost everyone was bailing the boat out, and the coxswain could feel the boat responding a little better.

He thought his fears about a rogue wave had been confirmed when a wall of gray became visible some distance off his port bow. He was greatly relieved when he recognized the shape as that of one of the fleet destroyers. Although he did not know it at the time, it was the destroyer that had provided the covering fire.

The lookouts on the destroyer had spotted the boat a little earlier, and the relieved captain had maneuvered his ship ahead of it to guide the boat back to its transport ship.

The cheers, grins, and wild waving coming from the demolition men as they passed the destroyer convinced the captain that they had been successful, and he informed the transport ship that, although he could see damage to the boat, all hands appeared to be alive and happy about something.

Shortly after they were hauled on board the transport ship, the badly shot-up Higgens boat was swung aboard. The crew counted thirteen major holes and numerous smaller holes. As they were inspecting the damage, the *Texas* steamed past heading for the river mouth.

Before dawn she had steamed up the mouth of the Wadi Sebou with her guns blazing into the stone fortress. The enemy replied with a fierce barrage, but the *Texas* crashed through what remained of the boom defenses and steamed into Port Lyautey. The assault troops raced ashore under the protective fire of the *Texas* and within hours had secured the airfield.

The members of the first Combat Demolition Unit were sent back to the United States and were used to assist in the formation of other Combat Demolition Units. The Navy had realized the need for such specialized teams, but they were still struggling to formulate a plan for their training and placement.

Seventeen determined men, with little training or experience, had shown what could be done. It was a start.

2

HISTORICAL DEVELOPMENT OF THE SEALS

The most elite fighting units of the United States Navy are the SEAL teams. They get their name from the environments in which they work: *SE*a, *A*ir, and *L*and. They are the Navy's specialists in unconventional warfare; or to quote official U.S. Navy terminology, they are "commissioned to conduct Naval Special Warfare."

The SEAL teams were commissioned on January 1, 1962, by the late President John F. Kennedy. They were a newly formed and organized unit with a specific mission role that had been devised as a result of the growing possibility of a conflict in Vietnam, and the possibility of similar conflicts arising in the future.

However, the mission role and origins of the SEALs stem from two sources—the primary one being the Underwater Demolition Teams (UDT) of the Navy and the secondary one being the Marine Corps Reconnaissance Units.

When amphibious assault landings are planned, several military organizations are utilized to provide intelligence information to the landing force commanders and the operations planners. In the latter stages of the planning, days or hours before the assault, two of these specialist organizations, the Marine Recon Units and the UDT, play a vital role in the prelanding preparations.

Briefly stated, the missions of these two organizations are as follows: the Marine Recon Units gather intelligence information from the water's edge landward and are divided into two basic groups—the Force Reconnaissance Company and the Battalion Reconnaissance Company, more usually called Force Recon and Battalion Recon. Both of these units are charged with reconnaissance of the landing area and the guidance of helicopters and other support aircraft and equipment into that area.

Their roles differ inasmuch as the Force Recon operates in four-man teams that are secretly landed well before either D-day or H-hour, and their intelligence reports are specifically for the landing force commander. They are very much a clandestine group, operating on foot and relying heavily on their concealment skills to survive. Force Recon personnel are trained underwater swimmers, inflatable boat handlers, and parachutists.

Battalion Recon follows Force Recon ashore, usually after the initial landings at H-hour. They operate as platoons or companies, and they gather intelligence information for their own battalion or task force group. They use helicopters and light motor vehicles for transport and rely upon speed and force size, rather than concealment, in the performance of their task. All Battalion Recon personnel are trained surface swimmers and boat handlers, and a few are trained in underwater swimming.

The mission role of the Underwater Demolition Teams is the reconnaissance and clearance of the assault beach landing area from the high-water line out to a depth of ten fathoms (sixty feet). Apart from surveying the beach and seaward areas, the UDT must remove obstacles—both natural (rocks and small reefs) and unnatural (mines, barbed wire, steel defense structures, and any other devices placed by the enemy as a deterrent to landing assault craft)—that might hinder the assault craft.

Additional tasks for the UDT are deep-water channel location and marking, assault craft guidance, landing and recovering guerillas and agents on enemy-occupied beaches, river and harbor penetration for the purpose of attacking sheltering ships, and the destruction of port facilities.

An Underwater Demolition Team comprises fifteen officers and one hundred men, and is organized into four operating platoons and one headquarters platoon. The complete team could operate as one unit, or it could be split up to operate in platoon size or smaller elements if required.

All UDT members are qualified underwater swimmers, parachutists, and inflatable boat handlers. They are also highly trained in deployment and retrieval techniques utilizing high-speed boats, submarines, low-flying helicopters, and parachuting from both helicopters and aircraft. Although the UDT does not normally operate inland, it is trained to do so, as the team could occasionally be called upon to operate in the hinterland for reconnaissance and demolition missions.

The success of the Marine Recon Units, particularly the clandestine Force Recon, and the UDT, has encouraged the Navy to form and develop a specialized team that could utilize the skills and functions of both. This unit was initially known as the Sea, Air, and Land Special Warfare Team; its primary skills were to be those of the UDT, with the addition of inland reconnaissance and various other specialized intelligence and operating functions.

All the original SEALs were UDT members, and present-day SEAL training commences with the basic UDT course. So it is to the UDT that we must look for the historical development of the SEALs.

In mid-1942, during World War II, the Allies planned Operation Torch. It was to be the opening of the Second Front or, more simply stated, the invasion of North Africa. One of three major amphibious landings was to be carried out on the west coast of Morocco, near the mouth of the Wadi Sebou River. A large cable and boom arrangement had been constructed by the enemy just inside the river mouth, preventing the Allies from gaining access to Port Lyautey and its airfield.

The Navy had hastily recruited a team of salvage experts and trained them for the sole purpose of destroying this boom. The seventeen-man team was officially named a Combat Demolition Unit, and it was basically the Navy's first organized SEAL/UDT. On November 11, 1942, this team successfully destroyed the Wadi Sebou River boom, and the Navy decided that a few more combat demolition teams would be a good idea. Nine days later, an incident was to occur that would give the Navy a painful reminder that combat demolition teams were required almost immediately.

November 20, 1942, was D-day on the Japanese-held island of Tarawa. The amphibious assault by the Marines was almost a total disaster when the landing craft ground to a halt on a submerged reef several hundred yards offshore. The Marines, laden with combat equipment, were forced to disembark into the water; and it was wrongly assumed that the water depth was very shallow all the way to the beach. As they wadded toward the land, the Marines were well within the range of enemy guns, and the barrage of fire took its toll.

However, an even greater toll was being taken by the sea as Marines stumbled into cracks, crevices, and deep holes. Hundreds of men drowned attempting to reach the shore, and it was confirmed after the battle that more men were drowned during the amphibious assault than were killed by the enemy.

The Navy and Marine chiefs of staff in the Pacific Theater became painfully aware of the fact that not only did they need a method of clearing obstacles from the landing area, but they also needed to have the capability to conduct more detailed reconnaissance of landing beaches. As a result of the disaster at Tarawa, it was decided that such tasks could only be performed by specially trained demolition teams, and the Navy started to think very seriously about accelerating its program to organize and train such teams.

As the Pacific Fleet commanders started to address the problem, the Atlantic Fleet commanders were planning the invasion of Italy. The landings were scheduled for July 1943, and it was not until late April that someone realized another Tarawa was possible if precautions were not taken to clear any beach defenses that might be encountered at the proposed landing point of Scoglitti, Sicily. The planners also realized that this problem might arise again on other intended amphibious landings, specifically one that was being organized for the invasion of France.

On May 6, 1943, a directive was issued by Admiral Ernest J. King, Commander in Chief, U.S. Fleet and Commander of Naval Operations, that there was an "urgent requirement" for the formation of "Naval Demolition Units." The word "urgent" meant the upcoming landings in Sicily—the Navy did not want another Tarawa—and the word "requirement" meant the planned island-taking campaign in the Pacific, as well as the proposed invasion of France.

On the day the directive was issued, steps were taken to cover both requirements. To initiate plans for the long-term requirement, a telegram was sent to Lieutenant Commander Draper L. Kauffman, founder and commander of the Navy Bomb Disposal School. It instructed him to report in person to Washington, D.C.—immediately.

The second step was to take care of the Sicilian problem. The morning after Admiral King's directive, a senior officer arrived at the Dynamiting and Demolition School, Camp Perry, Virginia, and requested volunteers for the formation of the Naval Combat Demolition Unit. Thirteen men who were completing a course immediately stepped forward. A few days later the volunteers were on their way to the Naval Amphibious Training Base at Solomon Islands, Chesapeake Bay, Maryland. They were joined by other volunteers who were already demolition trained, and by Lieutenant Fred Wise from the Navy Construction Battalion.

Lieutenant Wise was appointed officer in charge, and the complete team was then given a high-speed course in underwater demolition and rubber boat handling. When the course was finished, the team, under the official title of the Naval Combat Demolition Unit, was shipped out to the Mediterranean for the invasion of Sicily.

The invasion took place on the morning of July 10, 1943, but the assault landing craft encountered no difficulties in getting to the beach, and the troops encountered no serious obstacles on the beaches. Consequently, the Combat Demolition Unit was not used in the initial phase, to the great frustration of its members.

After two days work clearing more channels and removing obstacles a little farther inland, the team, somewhat disappointed, was sent back home.

Most of this first group were returned to Fort Pierce, Florida, where they became instructors for Lieutenant Commander Kauffman, who had established the training camp for the now officially named, Naval Combat Demolition Unit.

* * *

Personnel for the Navy Combat Demolition Units were initially recruited from the Navy Construction Battalions, Kauffman's old command (Bomb and Mine Disposal), and a group that was already based at Fort Pierce, the Navy and Marine Scout and Raider Volunteers. All were in top physical condition and had considerable swimming experience.

Training of the first unit began at Fort Pierce in July 1943, and, based on the assumption that a human being is capable of ten times the physical endeavor that is normally expended, it was organized to be intensely physical. The Scouts and Raiders were good-natured rivals of the Combat Demolition Unit, and Kauffman's men learned a considerable amount from them. One thing that the Scouts and Raiders gave the Demolition Unit was the training week known as Motivation Week.

Kauffman had asked for their assistance in putting together a physical training course that was a week long, but he wished it to be an accelerated version of their own eight-week course. The Scouts and Raiders happily obliged, and the result was a week so grueling that forty percent of the volunteers were removed from the course by their own choice. Since that time, this one week is still responsible for a thirty to forty percent attrition rate (see chapter 5, SEAL Training).

Apart from pure physical training, beach-clearing techniques were practiced extensively with almost total emphasis on demolition. Swimming was also taught, but at that time the course requirement was only a two-hundred-yard swim. In the years to come that was to change drastically.

Combat swimmers were not a new idea. They had been used successfully in the early days of World War II by the Italians to plant limpet mines and explosive charges on Allied ships in Gibraltar harbor on the western end of the Mediterranean. The British had retaliated with swimmers of their own, and the first teams were initially trained to remove the charges that the Italians had placed on the Allied ships. Later, the British teams began to take offensive action against their Italian antagonists by returning the favor and sinking Italian shipping in a similar manner.

During those early days at Fort Pierce, swim fins and face masks were tried out, but they were rejected. The instructors who tried the fins did not receive instruction in their use, and they found that they all developed leg cramps while using them. Although they did not know it at the time, the problem lay with the instructors themselves—they were trying too hard, a common problem even with the best of swimmers when they first use swim fins. Apart from the cramps, it was also felt that fins would only get in the way when the swimmers were working on coral reefs and in the surf. The face masks were discarded on the grounds that men working from rubber boats would not need them. So the fins and masks were initially rejected and were not used until later in the war when members of the clandestine OSS (Office of Strategic Service) were assigned to the teams. The OSS men were experienced users of both devices and quickly taught their new colleagues how to use them correctly.

As Kauffman was starting to train his teams, Allied intelligence information on the German occupied coast of Europe, and in particular the area around Normandy, showed extensive beach defenses in the form of mines and concrete, steel, and barbed-wire obstacles. Kauffman was given details of these obstacles, although he did not know where they would be encountered, and intensive training on similar obstacles was carried out.

A large portion of the demolition teams' training was conducted in the Florida Everglades, amidst the mud and grime that is common in such an environment. However, the swamps of Florida also have an abundance of ferocious alligators, deadly snakes, and a variety of other creatures that are totally repugnant to most humans. Working and training for days and nights under such conditions produced a special breed of warrior—that is if he survived the course, both physically and mentally.

It is reasonably well known, but not well publicized, that there were quite a few casualties and some fatalities during those early days of training. All volunteers were made aware of the fact that the training was dangerous and could prove fatal, but most of the personnel who volunteered for the Combat Demolition Unit expected it to be that way—they were seeking something challenging to begin with.

Those men who managed to graduate from the course were formed into six-man teams, each comprising five enlisted men and one commissioned officer or petty officer. Further training continued with these six-man units in order to mold them into efficient teams. The majority of the six-man teams were then sent to England in preparation for the invasion of Normandy.

When they first arrived in England there was some confusion in the Allied command as to what to do with them before the invasion. They were first assigned guard and patrol duties, functions that few of the men really knew; moreover, what they had once learned they had almost forgotten. After weeks of frustration, the combat demolition officers managed to make themselves heard, and the teams were rounded up from their various outposts.

Training began in earnest for the Normandy invasion, and they finally shipped out for the Omaha and Utah Beaches. Losses were heavy on those two beaches—somewhere between seventy and eighty percent at Omaha, and in excess of thirty percent at Utah—but the Combat Demolition Units performed their duties and earned the praise of commanders and troops alike.

During the invasion of France, those combat demolition men who survived the ordeal had learned invaluable lessons on the beaches, and these were later put to good use during the Pacific campaigns of World War II. With little or no addition, the basic demolition tactics used at Normandy have remained in use until the present time, and they are a tribute to the men who devised them.

In the Pacific the concept of the six-man team was dropped on the recommendation of Admiral Richmond Kelly Turner, Commander of the Fifth Amphibious Force, and at that time a name change also came about. Turner was an avid supporter of the demolition teams, and his recommendations were based on the experience of Tarawa and his knowledge of warfare in the Pacific: he was tailoring the Combat Demolition Units for that area.

Instead of Navy Combat Demolition Units, they were to be called the Underwater Demolition Teams, with each team comprising one hundred men and thirteen officers, a structure that remained unchanged for almost forty years. Two or three of these teams made up a unit, and two or more units made up a squadron. All basic training and selection was still carried out at Fort Pierce, Florida; but it was followed after graduation by six weeks of advanced training on the island of Maui, Hawaii, and swimming was to become one of the key elements. The two-hundred yard requirement first went to six-hundred yards, and shortly afterwards was increased to a mile.

Maui virtually became the main base for all the UDT teams and operational planning for the Pacific area. After the first few island invasions by the Marines, the UDT missions became more or less standardized. A reconnaissance mission was normally carried out any time from four days before D-day up to dawn on D-day itself, and sometimes even as close as one hour before H-hour. Destroyer escorts were converted to become fast UDT personnel carriers, known as Attack Personnel Destroyers. Each destroyer would carry four fast-landing craft that would be dropped just a few miles off the invasion beach. The fast-landing craft would be lowered with the UDT on board, and as these craft came within a thousand yards of the beach, a seven-man rubber boat would be slung over the port side.

The landing craft would then make a fast turn to port and run parallel to the beach at high speed, keeping its starboard side to the beach. Once the turn was made to parallel the beach, the craft was termed to be on its "splash run"; the swimmers would then drop into the rubber boat, one at a time on the concealed port side, in preparation for entering the water.

When the signal was given, the first man would drop into the water from the bouncing rubber boat, and his place would immediately be taken by the next man who would, in turn, wait for his signal to enter the water. In this way a line of swimmers could be dropped quickly at predetermined intervals along the entire length of the assault beach.

With barely their heads showing, the individual team members were almost impossible to spot from the beaches, even through binoculars, and they were rarely fired upon.

Once in the water the individual swimmers would swim in toward the beach surveying their assigned sections and writing the details down on plastic slates. With the survey completed they would swim back out to their starting point and again wait in a long line for the fast-moving boat with the rubber raft slung over the port side.

As the boat moved at high speed along the line, a crewman would be kneeling in the raft holding out a large padded loop or snare. It took good helmsmanship on the part of the boat's coxswain to guide his high-speed craft close to the man in the water, and good nerves on the part of the swimmer to carefully stay in one position as the craft came hurtling almost straight at him.

When the boat neared him the swimmer would extend his arm, and the crewman would hold the snare out to meet it. When the snare hit the swimmer's arm, he would immediately pull his hand in toward his chest locking the snare between his upper arm and forearm. The momentum of the speeding boat would cause the swimmer to be snatched quickly from the water and forced up over the side and into the rubber boat. The swimmer would then release the snare and quickly climb up into the landing craft, leaving the way clear for the crewman to snare the next swimmer.

If a swimmer was missed—and it was rare—he would have to wait until the boat finished its pickup run for the remainder of the line, when it would then return for him. No one liked second runs, as by this time the boat was usually receiving some enemy fire, and the enemy was being given time to work out range and speed.

Once the intelligence information gathered by the swimmers was assessed, the boats and swimmers would go into operation again—this time for demolition and clearance.

Items such as marker buoys and explosive charges would be dropped off with the individual swimmers. Swimmers on the extreme ends of the beach would run a long line of explosive detonating cord along the full length of the beach. The swimmers, who were placing charges on the individual obstacles, would then take their detonating cord to this main line and carefully attach it.

When all charges were attached the swimmers, except for those who were to set the fuses, would be picked up. On a given signal, the fuses were connected and set on time delays, and the remaining swimmers would quickly make their way out to sea for pickup. When the detonators finally exploded, the complete area would be cleared within half a second in one series of rippling explosions.

As the Marines moved from island to island, the UDT went with them; and the simple truth is that it was not the Marines who were the first to hit the beaches, it was always the UDT.

Almost all UDT activity during World War II was in the Pacific Theater, and by the end of the war there were some thirty-four teams in operation with a total complement of about 3,500 personnel.

The lessons learned on the beaches of Normandy served the UDT well. They are reflected in the casualty figures for the remainder of the war, which show that total losses in the UDT after the landings in France were a mere one percent.

The end of World War II brought about a massive reduction in UDT strength. The thirty-four teams were reduced to five, three of which were stationed with the Pacific Fleet and two with the Atlantic Fleet.

The outbreak of the Korean War in 1950 brought the UDT into action again and also brought about the development of new skills and techniques. Besides doing their traditional jobs of beach reconnaissance and clearance, the teams were called upon to assist in night demolition of enemy bridges, factories, railway tunnels, and a variety of other targets. They were also used to clear the heavily mined river and harbor entrances that were too restricted for conventional mine-sweeping operations.

The UDT method was unusual and extremely dangerous, but very effective. A line of swimmers would move into the harbor mouth, or river. As the swimmers came across a mine, they would attach an explosive charge with a time-delay fuse. Once a charge was placed, the swimmers would have to move on quickly as the shock wave that traveled through the water after the mine exploded would slam into their bodies with alarming violence and could easily incapacitate them. An unfortunate swimmer who was knocked out by a shock wave would almost certainly die.

Underwater Demolition Team One and Underwater Demolition Team Three were engaged in extensive operations in Korea. UDT One supplied a detachment to a unit of the British 41st Royal Marine Commando for a series of highly successful hit-and-run strikes along the northeastern coast of Korea. Personnel from UDT One were also used for further guerilla, commando, and inland reconnaissance operations behind enemy lines.

The hostilities in Korea were brought to a close in 1953. After the signing of the peace accord, UDT activities continued for a short time, with cleanup operations of harbors, beaches, and river entrances being the order of the day.

By the beginning of 1954, almost all UDT personnel had been removed from the Korean area, and on February 8 of that same year, UDT One was redesignated UDT Eleven. The reason for this redesignation is not exactly clear, particularly since there was no other military operational unit with a similar name. It seemed to be one of those mysterious changes that came about simply because someone wanted a change.

In February, 1955, the Nationalist Chinese decided to evacuate from the Tachen Islands. The U.S. Seventh Fleet was sent to support the withdrawal, and UDT Eleven was in action again charting safe channels and passages for the evacuation vessels. Once the islands had been cleared of their inhabitants, the UDT demolished all fortifications and munitions dumps to prevent the Chinese Communists from using them.

Between 1955 and the beginning of the Vietnam conflict in 1965, UDT members operated in many different areas of the world, performing a variety of tasks from searching for crashed military and civilian aircraft, surveying sites for the Defense Early Warning Radar system (DEW Line) in remote ocean areas and off the U.S. coast, and recovering astronauts and capsules after space shots. UDT members have always been the first personnel to have physical contact with the astronauts when they splash down in the sea on their return to earth.

Although the SEAL teams were actually commissioned as a separate unit in 1962, all their basic training was conducted with UDT. When the SEALs needed extra personnel for special missions, they were supplied by UDT, and the two units seemed to be almost inseparable.

The onset of the Vietnam conflict saw the UDT operating as a full team again, something that they had not done, except for training purposes, since the Korean War in 1953.

Subic Bay, in the Republic of the Philippines, became the headquarters for UDT operations in Vietnam. Thousands of miles of the Vietnam coastline were surveyed by the UDT swimmers, with one detachment operating from two submarines—the USS *Perch* and the USS *Tunney*. The submarines were specially modified to operate with the UDT, and there were two basic methods used to deploy the UDT members, mostly during the hours of darkness.

One method was to bring the submarine to a halt on the sea bed near the area to be surveyed; the swimmers would enter the water through air locks and swim toward the shore to complete their mission. The second method was for the swimmers to sit in a rubber boat on the deck of the submarine as it moved in toward the shore. At a predetermined point the submarine would submerge beneath the boat, leaving the swimmers to paddle the remaining distance to conduct their mission.

Apart from the extensive coastal area operations in Vietnam, UDT and SEALs, utilizing their skills of reconnaissance and demolition, onshore as well as offshore, also saw considerable action in the many river and delta areas of that nation. Some members of the UDT and SEALs actually spent more time far inland in the rivers of Vietnam than they did in their more traditional coastal environment.

UDT/SEAL operations during the Vietnam conflict were highly successful, just as they had been during all previous operations.

Today the UDT does not exist. As of October 1, 1983, they became SEALs. As SEALs, they will still carry out the UDT duties that they have performed so well in the past, as well as other specialized duties that they were occasionally used for.

For practical as well as security reasons, the amalgamation of the UDT into the SEALs was long overdue. It is a simple fact that in this world of rapidly advancing technologies, particularly those concerning conventional warfare, the less a nation's enemies or potential enemies know about its tactics and modes of operation, the more chance that nation has of successfully defending itself.

As far as reconnaissance and amphibious assault preparations are concerned, security leads to success, and the SEALs have always worked under the most strict security code.

3

BATTLEFIELD LOG:
Normandy, France—June 6, 1944

Naval Combat Demolition Unit Eleven was, quite logically, the eleventh team to qualify from Lieutenant Commander Kauffman's notorious training school in Fort Pierce, Florida. However, on November 1, 1943, the unit became the first fully trained Naval Combat Demolition Unit to set foot in England.

This unit was sent to England to prepare for the invasion of Europe, which was to commence with an amphibious landing on the beaches of Normandy; but Unit Eleven did not know that.

The unit comprised Lieutenant Lawrence Heideman and five men. When they arrived in the town of Plymouth, on the southern coast of England, they reported for duty at the operations office of the commander, Naval Forces Europe.

On the journey across the Atlantic, the six men had indulged in a warrior's favorite pastime, speculation, and their fertile minds had not yet exhausted all the possibilities when they arrived at the famous British Naval base in the Plymouth dockyards.

Fighting men speculate on what their orders are going to be for several reasons: it helps pass the time, it generates wagering, and if someone manages to guess correctly, it reduces the chance of being surprised. Warriors do not like surprises because in war the odds are almost completely in favor of the nasty surprise.

When they finally reported for duty, Lieutenant Heideman and his men were very surprised to discover that the commander of Naval Forces Europe did not know what a Naval Combat Demolition Unit was, and, obviously, if he did not know that, how could he possibly know what their mission was supposed to be.

To add to the confusion, nine more units arrived six weeks later, products of Kauffman's second training course, and they received the same surprise as Unit Eleven. The demolition men found themselves being separated from their team members and shipped to all parts of England for various duties totally unrelated to what they had been trained for.

The reason for the confusion was security. At that time, only a handful of top military men had official knowledge about the planned invasion of France, and only a few more knew of the real purpose of the Combat Demolition Units. However, the mess eventually got sorted out, and Lieutenant Robert Smith was placed in overall command of the Combat Demolition Units. The various members of the units were "retrieved" from their outposts in England and brought together at Falmouth for further training.

Practicing their demolition skills on existing beach defenses in England was out of the question—the British public would be outraged if they discovered their defenses against "Hitler's savage hordes" were being stripped because some fools wanted to practice blowing things up. Lieutenants Smith and Heideman were informed that if they wanted to practice blowing up beach obstacles, they would have to build their own—and they would also have to find their own materials to build them with.

At that time in England, when iron and steel were in such short supply that people were donating the fences and railings from around their beloved gardens for the war effort, gathering materials was not easy. The Combat Demolition Units went on the "scrounge," aided by the U.S. Army Fifth Corps Special Engineer Task Force, and many a concrete and steel roadblock disappeared from under the noses of the men who were guarding them.

Eventually, the demolition units managed to procure information, in the form of pictures and drawings, of the most difficult of the German beach defenses. The most dreaded of these defenses was Element C, which was known by the popular name of "the Belgian gate," because it resembled the gate that Belgian farmers seemed to have a passion for. These were massive steel gates of bolted and welded construction. They were some ten feet square and were held erect by a large framework assembly of similar construction. The estimated weight of the gates was three tons, and they were usually placed in the water at the lowest possible tide to afford maximum concealment. The gates were somewhat portable and had been designed in such a manner that they could be rolled down into the water at the last possible moment.

When the gates were first seen on aerial reconnaissance photographs, they were stacked in long lines a short distance inland from the beaches. They presented quite a puzzle to the intelligence officers, who originally assumed that they were part of a land defensive system. Their real purpose was not discovered until secret agents in France learned that the gates would be pushed into the sea, by forced peasant labor, just prior to an attempted invasion.

The realization that such a portable beach defensive system existed totally alarmed the Allied planners. If a landing craft were to hit one of these gates, it would certainly become impaled and useless, and it could also block a vital section of any landing beach. It was this discovery that had prompted the urgent request to Admiral King for trained demolition units, and it is hard to believe that when the demolition men first arrived in England they were not allowed to be informed about these defenses.

When the demolition men finally managed to construct a series of Belgian gates on their assigned practice beach, they soon discovered that the engineers who designed them knew what they were about. The gates were not easy to clear. Placing a bunch of explosives around them produced a tangled mess that was just as bad as the original object. Increasing the amount of explosives, in an attempt to blow the structures into tiny, unrecognizable pieces, was a good idea, but it was not acceptable because flying pieces of steel would endanger both the demolition men and any Allied troops that were on the beach.

Lieutenant Carl Hagensen was instrumental in solving the problem. He designed an explosive pack made from canvas that was easily handled by one man and would limit the blast to a controlled zone. The pack was loaded with one of the new plastic explosive compounds called C-2. Detonators were installed when the pack was made up, and a tail of another new product, a waterproof explosive detonating fuse called primacord, was left trailing from the pack.

On the outside of the pack a metal hook was attached to one end, and a short length of rope was attached to the other. This allowed the pack to be fastened quicky to the

gates, and the primacord simply had to be tied with an ordinary knot to the main fuseline. Sixteen of these packs, when
placed correctly on a gate, would blow the supporting structure away, and the gate would simply fall flat.

Lieutenant Hagensen's name was to become known
throughout the Navy demolition teams, and it still is; his
invention was an extremely easy way to transport and attach
a considerable amount of explosives to a variety of obstacles. Much later in the war, when the Navy ordnance manufacturers started to supply similarly made-up packs, they
were given the official designation, "Hagensen packs."

By February, the ten Combat Demolition Units had
been split into three groups for further training—two
groups were based at Fowey and Salcombe on the southern
coast of England, and one was based at Swansea in Wales.
Toward the end of February eight more demolition units
arrived from Fort Pierce, and they were divided between
the three temporary bases.

It was late March and all the units were preparing to
gather at a designated marshalling area in readiness for the
invasion, when a sudden change in plans occurred. The Allied planners had just been supplied with intelligence information and aerial photographs that showed a considerable
increase in activity in the German coastal defense program.
Further construction was taking place, particularly in the
region of the beaches at Normandy where the Allies were
intending to land.

This evidence, at such a late date, caused a great deal of
consternation in the high command. They had not planned
for such heavy beach defenses, and the planners went
scurrying around to find demolition experts they knew they
had somewhere. The men of the Naval Combat Demolition
Unit suddenly discovered they were now on the popularity
list, and it meant more training. Kauffman was ordered to

send all the available men he had, and sixteen units suddenly found themselves on their way to England.

When the intelligence details of the newly constructed beach defenses were passed to the Fifth Corps Special Engineer Task Force, to which the Combat Demolition Units were attached, both Army and Navy men alike were horrified. One look at the information told them that there were so many obstacles below the high water mark that thirty-four–six-man Navy teams were not enough.

Apart from their sheer number, the obstacles were more varied than the engineers or Navy demolition had been told. Besides the Belgian gates at or below the water marks, there were rows of steel and concrete antitank tetrahedrons, jagged hedgehogs, and other devices, some of which had actually been designed by the great German tank commander, Field Marshal Erwin Rommel, who was then Hitler's inspector of beach defenses. There were also rows of mines, both antitank and antipersonnel, buried in the sand and pebbles.

It was also discovered that mines had been placed on most of the Belgian gates, thus making the demolition unit's task even more difficult. When they were informed that there was a tidal change of twenty-five feet, and that once the tide started to move it went from low water to high water in less than three and a half hours, the Navy men became alarmed. They pointed out the problems they would have trying to clear such a vast array of obstacles below the high water mark. As a direct result, the already troubled invasion planners in Allied headquarters changed the date of the invasion in order that the tides would be favorable for the Navy Combat Demolition Units.

To solve the manpower problems, the existing six-man unit was first reorganized into five-man units, giving a total of forty-units. Each unit was then increased in size with the addition of three U.S. Navy seamen recruited from bases in

Scotland, and five U.S. Army combat engineers. These thirteen-man units were led by the Navy officers, and they were called "Gap Assault Teams." Each Gap Team was then assigned a further twenty-six men from the Army engineers under an Army lieutenant, and their responsibility was to clear the obstacles from the high-water mark landward, while the Navy-led team took care of the tide zone obstacles. The Navy teams would have available the usual rubber boats, and the Army engineer teams were assigned two tanks and either a bulldozer or a tank with a bulldozer blade attached ("tankdozer"). The assault plan called for tanks and infantry to land ahead of the demolition teams and set up to provide covering fire as the teams cleared the beaches.

All this was arranged at a four-day, high-ranking conference with Army engineers in the last week of March, and pandemonium ensued as the teams were restructured and increased in size. By the second week in April, all the thirteen-man Navy teams were assembled at Appledore, Devon, on the southwest coast of England for further training. Everyone worked overtime to train the new Navy and Army additions. By May 22, all their planned training was completed, and the teams moved to their final staging area in Salcombe, where their primary task was the manufacture of ten thousand much-needed Hagensen packs.

The teams, totaling some 550 men, were now split into two groups—one for Omaha Beach and the other for Utah Beach. Commanders of higher rank were appointed to give the units more credibility and authority. Captain Thomas Wellings was given the command of the Omaha group, and Lieutenant Commander Herbert Peterson took command of the Utah group. Both had been given intensive instruction by Kauffman at Fort Pierce before they took over their new commands.

Until the beginning of April, the Navy demolition men had been training in traditional combat uniform, swimming included; but new intelligence information was flooding into Allied headquarters almost every minute, and some of it was to bring about an unwelcome change of battle dress for the Normandy landings.

The Allied high command began to believe that the Germans had some fiendish tricks waiting for the invasion forces. Stories that mustard gas and poison gas, some much worse than the then most recently developed lewisite—a blistering poison gas named after W. L. Lewis, the American chemist who concocted it in 1919—would be used against the Allied invaders. There were rumors that mines filled with such gases were in place on the beaches, and that some of the mines were triggered to release a flood of gasoline onto the surface of the sea. Once the floating gasoline was ignited, the ensuing inferno was obvious.

The Allied commanders could not take the chance that such tactics and devices would not be used, and as their now vital demolition teams were to be some of the first on the beaches, they had to have adequate protection. Gas masks were issued to take care of one problem, and flame-resistant firemens' suits were issued to take care of the possibility of the sea being fired with gasoline.

None of this was helpful to the Combat Demolition Units. They were still expected to wear combat dress underneath the cumbersome suits, and that made movement even more difficult. Add to that the fact that each man had almost ninety pounds of equipment—most of it explosive charges—to carry and it becomes obvious that speed and agility were greatly reduced.

However, the tough training that Kauffman had put his men through was now beginning to pay off. The Army engineers just could not quite keep up with the Navy demolition men, and neither could some of the units' new seamen recruits.

On June 1, the group for the Utah Beach left for the

marshaling area, and on June 3 the Omaha group traveled to Portland Harbor, Dorset, to board its transport ships.

When the greatest armada of all times mustered at their assigned points in the English Channel, almost everything was going according to plan. British and American intelligence officers knew that they had deceived the enemy as to their exact landing point; the complete invasion force had moved out exactly as planned—part had been out at sea for several days—and every vessel seemed to be in its correct place right from the start. There was just one thing wrong: the weather was atrocious. No invasion force should have left harbor under such conditions, but there had already been several postponements and another one was simply out of the question.

The raging seas and howling wind battered and tore at the assault ships and landing craft as they fought their way across the English Channel. It was an almost identical storm in the same region, some 376 years previously, that had shattered the great Spanish Armada that was about to attack England. This storm on June 6, 1944, did not destroy the Allied Armada, but it did exact its toll.

Ships began to flounder in the heavy seas as they took on more water than they could handle, and some had to be abandoned and left to the escorting rescue tugs. By the time the armada reached the French coast, the majority of the troops in the open-decked vessels were cold, tired, and seasick. Those who had to transfer from the larger ships into the smaller craft for the first part of the assault were faced either with a harrowing ride into the water in the boats that were lowered from davits, or with the misery of crawling down the cargo nets and trying to jump into pitching and tossing assault craft. Either method produced nerve-racking and unpleasant experiences.

The plan for the Omaha and Utah Beaches was that the

first wave of assault craft would comprise amphibious tanks and assault craft carrying infantry, and the second wave would carry the demolition teams. The tanks and infantry were to land and establish the beachhead, and they would then provide covering fire for the combined Naval Combat Demolition Units and Army engineers to clear channels through the Belgian gates and other obstacles.

Once the Gap Assault Teams had cleared the beach obstacles, the larger ships could move in and land the reinforcing troops and heavy equipment. As the larger vessels were disgorging their contents, the demolition teams would continue to clear more channels through the gates, or clear wrecked landing craft from existing channels.

The first problem arose off Omaha Beach when most of the new amphibious tanks started to sink almost as soon as they rolled out of their transport ships. The sea conditions were just too rough for them to survive. The second problem was that the preinvasion bombardment, both aerial and naval, had been directed too far inland. Some of the enemy reserves and their communications installations had been destroyed, but the coastal defenses—particularly the big 88-mm and 155-mm guns—were still operational.

The German gunners of the 726th Infantry Regiment, who were manning the coastal guns, were professionals. They systematically started to destroy the landing craft of both infantry and demolition units and the remaining amphibious tanks with their powerful 88-mm coastal guns, as soon as the vessels came within a half mile of Omaha Beach.

As a result, only a few amphibious tanks landed, and they became stuck almost immediately on a steep, pebbled bank just above the high-water mark. What remained of the first infantry units and the demolition teams landed at the same time. Almost immediately, the demolition men shed their firemens' suits and gas masks and went about their assigned tasks. Enemy bullets and bombs were the only things they had to worry about; there was no flaming sea or poison gas.

One demolition team managed to clear its first assigned section of the gates within about twenty minutes, despite the fact that most of the obstacles had antipersonnel mines attached. The time was good; but out of the thirteen-man team, four were dead and another four seriously wounded. It was much the same with the other teams, but their problems were only just beginning.

The first assault wave became bogged down on the beach under heavy enemy fire, and as more troops landed they sought cover—behind the very defenses the demolition teams were trying to clear. Primacord lines were tripped-over and torn from their charges; wounded and bleeding demolition men, both Navy and Army, almost fought with their own infantry to get them to move. They even helped carry infantry wounded away from the obstacles before they blew them up.

As more infantry landed the situation became even worse. Everyone seemed to want to hide behind the obstacles that were packed with explosives, and the German snipers were picking off the demolition men who seemed to be the only ones moving on Omaha Beach.

Tanks in the second wave of the assault started to fire at their own troops; shells from the Naval bombardment fell short and, at one point, it seemed that only the enemy knew the right direction to shoot in.

Most of the assigned bulldozers or tankdozers did not get ashore when they were supposed to, thus making life even more difficult farther up the beach. Some of the landing craft carrying the demolition explosives were blown out of the water before they reached the beaches and that created more problems.

Sadly, yet remarkably because of the enemy's strength, only five channels out of the required sixteen were cleared on the first assault. However, as the tide subsided that afternoon, the remnants of the demolition units went back into action to clear more gaps, and also to clear some of the new obstacles—their own wrecked landing craft.

At the end of the day over sixty percent of the Navy Combat Demolition Teams were on the casualty lists for Omaha Beach. The remainder, though near exhaustion, were still at work clearing the beaches.

On Utah Beach the situation had been a little better, mainly because of an error in navigation that caused the first assault wave to land a mile farther to the southeast than was originally planned. This area was less heavily defended than the designated one, otherwise the losses would have been as bad as on Omaha.

The tanks and infantry landed as planned, and provided cover for the thirteen-man demolition teams. The teams were initially without the support of the Army engineers as they had been delayed due to an error in timing. However, when they did arrive, they promptly completed their part of the operation. Problems with the infantry using the beach obstacles as cover were not as severe as at Omaha, but they were troublesome. No tanks or Naval artillery fired into the soldiers on the Utah Beaches; but the enemy did enough damage, and the demolition teams' casualty figures stood at thirty percent when darkness fell.

When the beaches had been cleared and the enemy driven back, the casualties—wounded, dead, and missing—were listed. Almost all those Navy Combat Demolition Unit members who were missing eventually turned up: some, days later; some, weeks later. It would appear that their ordeal on the beaches had not deterred them—they had all gone inland to continue fighting alongside the infantry after they had finished their work on the beaches. Several of them were recommended for decorations by senior Army commanders who had watched them assist by destroying enemy-held pillboxes, gun emplacements, bunkers, and roadblocks far inland.

The Navy Combat Demolition Unit came away from the Normandy invasion battered and bloodied. The men had lost over forty-five percent of their number; but they had performed the tasks that they had been trained for, and they had established themselves as a necessary part of future amphibious landings.

They had discovered that all the new explosives they had tried had worked well, and that most of their demolition techniques were correct. They had discovered the value of the strenuous training that Draper Kauffman had put them through. And they had discovered that they could not work with infantry milling around them. In the future, they would request that they do their job without infantry support, as they felt it would be easier if they were alone and unarmed.

As they came away from Normandy, they did not realize that they would never again function as they had on the beaches of France. They were the first and only members of the Navy to see this kind of action under the name of the Navy Combat Demolition Unit. Back at Fort Pierce, Kauffman was already organizing a name change and a change in methods of operation. This was as a result of recommendations put forward by Admiral Richmond Turner and Captain Tom Hill, both of whom had firsthand experience in the disastrous amphibious landings at Tarawa.

The lessons that had been learned on the Normandy beaches were not to be forgotten, but the manner in which they were learned would. The Navy Combat Demolition Unit was to become the Navy Underwater Demolition Team, and in the future the men would work from small boats and in the water itself. They were to refine their skills to such an extent that they would never again experience the casualty figures they had suffered during the breaching of Hitler's self-proclaimed Atlantic Wall.

4

BATTLEFIELD LOG:
Omaha Beach, Normandy—June 6, 1944

As a gunner's mate, William ("Bill") Freeman had been a member of the first Navy Combat Demolition Unit that had destroyed the cable and boom defenses in the Wadi Sebou River in French Morocco. Freeman had been the inventor and builder of the massive underwater incendiary bomb that served as an excellent morale booster after the first aborted attempt on the river defenses, even though it was not used in the raid, except as jettisonable ballast.

Freeman was also a member of the first class to undergo training under Lieutenant Commander Kauffman at Fort Pierce, Florida. And, as a chief petty officer, he was in the first six-man team, under the command of Lieutenant Heideman, to be sent to England in preparation for Operation Overlord—the Normandy invasion.

When the final restructuring of the Combat Demolition Units took place, just prior to the invasion, Freeman was second in command of the thirteen-man Gap Assault Team under Lieutenant Heideman. However, in the final days prior to the commencement of Operation Neptune (the amphibious phase of Operation Overlord), Heideman was given the overall responsibility for the demolition work on the right flank of Omaha Beach. Freeman was then promoted to team leader, and another seaman was added to his assault team to bring the team up to strength.

On the cross-channel trip, Freeman and the Army lieutenant in charge of the twenty-six man Army engineer team held a two-man conference. The official plan required that each Army/Navy team clear a gap fifty yards wide through the beach defenses. The thirteen-man Navy team was assigned the job of clearing Element C (the Belgian gates) and any other obstructions from the low-water mark to the high-water mark, and the Army team was assigned the clearing of all the obstructions from the high-water mark to the top of the beach.

Chief Freeman had been thinking, and he suggested to the Army lieutenant that they change the official plan, just a little. He reasoned that, as it would be low tide when they landed on Omaha Beach, all the obstacles would be clear of the water, and everyone would be working under reasonably dry conditions. When the tide started to rise, it would come in fast, approximately one foot of rise every eight or nine minutes. That might not seem too fast, but, in reality, because of the gently sloping beach at Omaha, the water would be moving toward the shore very quickly indeed. Freeman doubted that his thirteen-man team could get all the obstacles properly charged before the racing water covered everything up. He suggested that the Army engineer team take care of the more important seaward obstacles as he felt the twenty-six man team could do the job in about twenty minutes without anyone getting his feet wet. His thirteen-man team would start on the obstacles from the high-water mark and work landward. They would continue placing charges until the Army team had reached the high-water mark. At that point they would stop, regardless of how many charges the Navy team had placed on the landward obstacles, and fire every change that had been placed. This would ensure that the assigned fifty-yard gap between the high- and low-water marks, which would be underwater within an hour, would be clear to accept the larger landing craft carrying the assault troops. With the tide-zone obstacles cleared, both teams could then work together in clearing the landward obstacles. They could do this more or less at their leisure, as the infantry should have taken care of any nearby enemy.

To add weight to his suggestion, Freeman also pointed out that a twenty-six-man team working on a fifty-yard front above the high-water mark presented a much better target to the enemy snipers than a thirteen-man team.

The Army lieutenant, who was just as brave as Freeman, did not have to hear the last statement. He had seen the logic in Freeman's initial statements, and he readily agreed to swap the team roles. Both teams, having worked together during training, were well acquainted with each other's function, and, as everyone had practiced his demolition skills on the same type of obstacles, it took only a few minutes to inform the men and brief them on the change of plan. After the briefing the Navy men exchanged most of their Hagensen explosive packs for the more traditional military demolition charges, since the obstacles farther up the beach did not require the much larger pack explosives.

As the landing craft approached its assigned beach area on Omaha Beach, Freeman could see that things were wrong: he could not see the infantry that was supposed to be ahead of the demolition teams. He could just see one of the amphibious tanks as it started to clear the water on its way up the beach; he knew it would not get very far among the obstacles, but at least it had arrived and would provide some covering fire. As he looked around, he could see nothing but chaos; the enemy had not been "bombed and shelled out of existence," as Freeman and his men had been informed before their landing craft departed from its staging point offshore.

Nothing could have been further from the truth, as 88-mm shells were landing in salvos of three all around them. Long lines of heavy machine-gun tracer shells streaked out from the high ground at the top of the beach and buried themselves in both the sea and the approaching rows of landing craft. Freeman watched several craft take direct hits and suddenly veer away from the beach, while others just stopped and began to wallow drunkenly about in the heavy seas. The enemy, it was plain to see, was very much in existence and was displaying considerably more fire power than even he had expected.

However, it was too late to worry now. Gaps had to be cleared to allow the Allied troops to drive the enemy back, otherwise the problems would only get worse.

The time on Freeman's watch showed 0633 hours when the landing craft shuddered to a halt just short of the beach. When the ramp was lowered, a hail of bullets peppered the inside of the boat as the men rushed to get out. When they left the ramp, they found the water was waist deep, and they struggled under the weight of their heavy explosive packs as they waded up onto the sand. Sniper fire was increasing considerably as Freeman led his men up through the rows of mined obstacles toward the high-water mark. As there were no tracks in the sand and no sign of the infantry, he now realized that his team was the first to set foot on that section of beach.

The Army engineers set to work on the Belgian gates near the water's edge as the Navy men reached the high-water-mark obstacles. The inshore obstacles, behind the gates, were a mixture of ramps and cruciform structures. The ramps were made by burying the end of a large timber post deep in the sand. The posts, some twelve to fourteen inches in diameter, were set at a shallow angle, with the buried end toward the waterline, so that they pointed upward in the form of a ramp toward the top of the beach. The top ends of the posts were approximately fifteen feet away from where they entered the sand, and they were supported either by a single vertical post, almost like a tree stump, or by two posts in the shape of an inverted V. As with the main ramp post, the supporting stumps, or inverted Vs, were buried deep in the sand, and they protruded about five feet above it. Large metal spikes, steel straps, and wire ropes were used to fasten the poles together, and for further effect a small mine was attached to the top of each ramp.

The primary purpose of the ramps was the destruction of landing craft, and to that end they were quite effective as many a boat crew was to discover. The smaller boats would run up a ramp and then topple over and capsize; the larger ones would ride the device to the top where the mine would explode and blow a hole in the bottom. The vessel, firmly impaled, would then be out of action and would simply become another obstruction.

The cruciform posts, which also had mines attached, were just another form of obstruction designed to make life difficult for the landing craft.

The obstacles known as hedgehogs were made from three steel beams fashioned in a form that resembled the framework of a simple tepee. These devices were about four feet high, and, like the other obstacles, they too had a mine attached to their tops. The hedgehogs were primarily an antitank, antivehicle device, but they were sometimes seen below the high-water mark.

The rows of hedgehogs were at the top of the beach, and, as Freeman and his men worked on the other defenses, they afforded a little protection from the enemy snipers. However, they were no protection against their own amphibious tanks, called DDs (Duplex Drive, propellers for water and tracks for land). The tanks were moving backward and forward along the sand, just below the high-water mark, and were firing over the heads of the demolition unit. In their attempt to provide covering fire for the team, the tank gunners were firing rather low and too close to the men trying to attach explosive charges. That would have been acceptable to Freeman if the enemy had not been shooting back, but he realized that the position the tanks were firing from was simply drawing attention not only to the tanks, but to his men as well. The very article that was supposed to protect them was more likely to get them killed. Freeman finally dropped his explosive packs and ran down to them. The tank commanders did not hear exactly what he said; but they saw the direction in which his finger was pointing, and they heard a considerable amount of profanity. The message was clear and they pulled away.

Freeman noted that the Army engineers were getting on quite well, and he returned to his team. One of his men was moving between two beach obstacles and was cut to pieces by an enemy machine gun. Moments later, two seaman members of his crew, who were assigned the task of bringing the spare explosives from the landing craft, were shot and wounded as they struggled through the surf. The Army engineer medic who ran to assist them was killed instantly by an enemy sniper. Another one of Freeman's men was shot in the leg, but he struggled on for a few minutes before being forced to stop. The Army team was not doing much better, men were being wounded and killed by sniper fire and shrapnel from the 88-mm guns.

By now the tide was on the rise and racing across the sand as Freeman had suspected it would, but the engineers managed to stay ahead of it. Freeman was carefully placing a small charge around a mine on one of the obstructions (all the mines had to have a separate charge attached as destroying the obstacle did not ensure that the mine would explode), when he too was hit; but he said nothing and continued to work. Shortly afterward another member of his team was badly wounded and died within a few minutes.

The Army team finished loading the gates and several rows of low-water obstructions on schedule. They fired the purple smoke signal that warned of an impending detonation and everyone, including Freemen and his remaining men, threw themselves flat on the beach. The ensuing explosion shook the beach and hurled sand and debris high in the air. When the debris settled, the jagged gates and the seaward obstacles could no longer be seen, and both teams went back to work.

The Navy men were working on the remaining obstacles backward from the land toward the water, and the engineers were working toward them from the sea. Several more men were killed and wounded as the two teams brushed shoulders on the last row of obstacles. The loss of their colleagues seemed to drive the remaining men to work even harder, and between setting charges they would occasionally check on the wounded.

The loading of all the obstacles was completed just a few minutes ahead of the advancing tide. Gunner's mate Bob Bass worked quickly reeling out the main primacord line and attaching the explosive pack leads to it as he passed each obstacle. When he had all the charges attached, he fastened the waterproof detonator to the end and looked to Chief Freeman for the signal to fire. Freeman signaled NO! and pointed down the beach.

Bob Bass had been so intent with his work that he had not seen the infantry come ashore. The infantry was late because its landing craft had been late leaving the line of departure; and on the way to the beach, it had been delayed even further when the craft drifted badly off course. The coxswain, instead of dumping the men on a beach that was not assigned, as a lot of coxswains did, gallantly braved the enemy shells and moved along the coast until he located the correct beach. He was not aware that the time delay was going to cause hardship to the demolition teams. The infantry, mostly unseasoned troops, had gone through a nightmare ride to get to the beach; and when the ramp on the landing craft was lowered, the troops were greeted by a hail of fire.

As they waded through the surf toward the beach, with bullets slapping the water around them and their fellow soldiers being cut down, they instinctively sought cover behind anything that was higher than six inches. With the enemy gunners shelling and raking the beach with rifle and machine-gun fire, the beach obstacles appeared as a haven to the terrified soldiers.

Chief Freeman and the Army lieutenant ran among the charged obstacles shouting and roaring at the soldiers and pointing to the explosive packs. The bewildered infantry must have thought they were madmen to be standing up with bullets and shrapnel flying around them. The chief and the lieutenant stopped pleading with those who would not move and started to kick them. When the raw troops finally got the message, they regained their composure and displayed their courage by following the example of Freeman and the lieutenant in helping their wounded colleagues and the wounded demolition men farther up the beach to what was questionably called safety.

When he was satisfied that there were no more living soldiers among the obstacles, Freeman gave the order to Bass. The gunner's mate fired the purple warning flare, pulled the fuse, and raced up the beach. He had barely dived flat beside the chief and the lieutenant when a shuddering blast demolished the remaining obstacles and hurled their fragmented parts in all directions.

When the last shower of sand had fallen around them, the remains of the Army and Navy team looked up to see a clean fifty-yard swath all the way down the beach. Chief Freeman looked at his watch—it was 0655 hours, just twenty-two minutes since they had hit the beach, and the first part of their mission had been accomplished.

The tide continued to race in as Freeman, Bass, and several others went out into the water to install the green channel markers that would indicate a clear passage for the incoming assault craft. On the way back to the shore, Bass and one of the Army engineers went to assist the two seamen who had been injured when they were bringing up the spare explosives. The men had been lying by the water's edge beside the dead Army medic since they had been hit shortly after landing. As they moved slowly up the beach the Army engineer was killed, and Bass, who was assisting the other wounded seaman, was hit in the shoulder by a piece of shrapnel from an exploding 88-mm shell. Bass kept going, dragging the wounded man with him. Freeman picked up the other seaman from beside the dead engineer and carried him up the beach.

The chief ordered everyone to make for a steep shingle bank farther up the beach. The men worked their way slowly toward it, dragging and carrying the wounded, with the enemy snipers trying desperately to wipe them out. When they reached the bank, they were much less of a target for the snipers, and Freeman made them dig a deep trench in the pebbles and sand to provide further protection. It was not until they started digging that they realized they were in the middle of an enemy minefield. They looked at one another, shrugged their shoulders, and, being demolition men, carefully placed the mines they had discovered to one side. When the trench was finished, Freeman had it lined with kapok and inflated lifebelts. He then placed the wounded on them.

Two landing craft approached the gap the teams had blown and were hit by salvos of 88-mm shells. Both exploded in flames and sank, and, to the further dismay of the demolition men, they almost blocked the channel.

Throughout the remainder of the morning and most of the afternoon, the enemy continued shelling and machine gunning the beach as more and more troops painfully made their way up from landing craft that managed to make it through the safe channels. Except for Freeman, who was continuously crawling away and checking for survivors and wounded men, the demolition men could do nothing but watch.

When the tide went out in the late afternoon, Freeman gathered together his uninjured men and took them around the beach to gather up packs of unused explosives. He managed to get some from Engineer units that were moving inland, and he raided wrecked landing craft that were drifting ashore. He then found a bulldozer and two amphibious tanks that were, amazingly, still working.

With this assortment of equipment and personnel, he managed to clear another fifty-yard section alongside the one he had cleared in his first twenty minutes on the beach. That done, he set about clearing some of the wrecked landing craft and burned-out tanks that were blocking sections of the beach.

During the demolition work, Freeman was constantly looking for any craft that was going back out to the battleships and cruisers lying offshore. He was seeking passage for his wounded men, but, due to the shortage of available vessels, it was 1900 hours before he managed to get the men off the beaches.

At the close of day, Freeman's team of twelve was reduced to four able-bodied men. Four had been killed and the remaining four were wounded. The Army engineer team that had worked with them had been similarly reduced: only seven men remained in action.

Chief Freeman then "disappeared" for three weeks. He was last seen helping some engineers at the top of the beach before they went inland with the infantry. He reappeared some three weeks later, on June 22, having returned from an unauthorized "blasting spree" with the advancing allied army.

He had indulged in the highly frowned upon, but time-honored, sailor's habit of going along with the troops, just to help out.

When he arrived back at the beaches, the Allies had constructed the famous temporary port, the Mulberry harbor.

Mulberrys were simply large, enclosed concrete caissons that were floated into position and then flooded until they settled on the seabed. Two days before he returned, on June 20, a violent storm had created havoc with the harbor, and there were wrecked ships and Mulberrys strewn up and down the beach.

As he was trying to hitch a ride back to England, he was spotted by the harbormaster who had been a beach landing officer during the invasion. The man knew of Chief Freeman's demolition skills—he had seen the result of his work—and since good demolition men were almost impossible to get, he used his rank and ordered Freeman to stay and clear up the beach. The chief protested, explaining that he was long overdue and did not want to get into more trouble. The harbormaster understood and struck a deal with him.

Freeman remained on the beaches for two weeks assisting with the cleanup. When he arrived back in England, he reported for duty with a neatly typed and signed report of his "official" activities during his absence. The signature was that of the harbormaster, and it was not questioned.

When he had submitted his report, he was informed that he had been awarded the Navy Cross, and then, to his apparent horror, he was informed that he was to be commissioned. All he was reported to have said was, "What a blow!"

5

SEAL TRAINING

Probably the most difficult thing to do with an elite fighting group, particularly one with a role similar to that of the SEALs, is to allow the men to retain their individuality and, at the same time, maintain the absolute discipline that is essential in any front-line military organization. It is a problem that has been faced many times by such groups as the rangers, the Special Forces, the British commandos, and the British Special Air Service Regiments.

All of these groups, including the SEALs, rely heavily upon discipline, teamwork, individual physical ability, and the intelligence of their members. The basic problem is that there is no real order of significance for these four criteria—the standards must be high in all four areas.

Experience has shown that if men of average or better intelligence and common sense are selected, then the remaining criteria can be satisfied by judicious training. The SEALs start their selection in this manner, but today, unlike years ago, no individual is actively recruited. All of its members are volunteers from within the U.S. Navy and must have a minimum of two and a half years left to serve. Apart from a steady flow of applications from ambitious individuals, the SEALs do occasionally go on recruiting drives, but in a strange manner. Word somehow leaks out that more men are required, which seems to stir the minds of all sorts of individuals, and the applications pour in.

Despite the fact that there are rigid initial requirements that have to be met before applications are sent in, some ninety percent of all applications received are politely rejected—most on the grounds that there are no vacancies. For those whose initial applications are accepted, there is further screening in the form of interviews and background checks for security reasons; this produces another batch of rejections, again as high as ninety percent. That apparently leaves very few men, but exact numbers are not known. Security starts at the very beginning, and it appears that no one man on the selection board knows the precise number of initial applicants.

Those individuals who are finally selected are eventually given a date to report for final selection and basic training, called BUD/S (Basic Underwater Demolition/ SEAL), at the Navy Amphibious Warfare School in Coronado, California. At this point the selection officers have chosen, to the best of their ability, a group of potential candidates based only on an assessment of intelligence, common sense, attitude, military record, and state of health. It is now up to their colleagues in the training school to find out if the recruits—officers and men alike—have the credentials that they, the recruits, think they have.

The first thing that is pointed out to all the recruits is that they were not invited; they invited themselves, and as such, they can leave and return to their old units anytime they so choose, day or night, and there will be no mention of it on their records. They are informed that they do not have to obey any order they are given; if they think that something is too dangerous, they do not have to do it; and, finally, they may complain about anything they so choose. Once all this has been said, the volunteers are then told that failure to obey any order, instruction, or command, or to voice any complaint, will instantly assure them a ticket back to wherever they came from.

Hard, enforced physical training tests more than a man's physical ability: that is the secret of SEAL training. It tests his mind, his will to continue when he feels his body can take no more. As SEAL training is based on the premise that the human body can take more than ten times that which is normally considered possible, it extracts more than even the fittest volunteer knew was possible.

The first two weeks of training are not really the start of the SEAL course. They are called "indoctrination weeks" and are used for further selection procedures.

Contrary to what some people think, they are not the worst of the entire twenty-five week course, despite the fact that the working day is fifteen hours long and is almost all physical. The SEAL instructors build up gradually, increasing the pace day by day, conditioning the men for what they know is to come if the volunteers get through the first two weeks. Apart from long runs, miles of swimming, commando-style assault courses, and various forms of exercises, there are brief respites for classroom courses in apparently mundane subjects such as first aid, signaling, mathematics, etc.

Swimming training is started, without the use of aids such as swim fins, and the volunteers learn the strokes that the SEALs have found best suited to their needs. Drown-proofing techniques are taught, with the real test coming when men are thrown into the water with their hands and feet tied. The first swimming test is to cover three hundred meters in eleven minutes, but that's just a start.

During the first two weeks, the volunteers are treated infinitely worse than raw recruits entering even the toughest of infantry units. They are goaded, harassed, and intimidated with apparent maliciousness. The instructors are watching for even the slightest trace of retaliation, resentment, or anger—such personal traits cannot be tolerated in the SEALs, particularly when they are under pressure.

By the end of the first two weeks, further reviews are carried out, and the original group of volunteers is trimmed down a little. In order to ensure that everyone is assessed fairly, instructors are rotated amongst the trainees, and no one instructor can call for the removal of a volunteer; all the instructors must agree. Some men will have already dropped out of their own free will; others who might have made it are removed because of training injuries, such as sprains, torn muscles, broken bones, and severe lacerations. These men are usually permitted to reenter the first available training course as soon as their injuries have mended. Those who have been removed because they were considered unsuitable are returned to their original units with no shame attached, but they are not permitted to reapply for the SEALs.

With the two weeks of testing or indoctrination completed, the remaining volunteers now move into the first phase of training. The level of physical endeavor is increased and the pace is quickened day by day. The instructors seem less patient, and life becomes one continuous struggle, both physically and mentally—physically to complete the work, and mentally to force the body to do it. The trainees are constantly being told, "It is mind over body, nothing more, just mind over body." All the telling in the world does not seem to help, the tasks just seem to get more difficult, but, strangely enough, they get completed.

The men are split up into six-man teams and are given

a seven-man inflatable life raft to train with. The raft comes complete with paddles, repair kit, first-aid box, and spare ropes, and must be kept in perfect working order. It weighs about three hundred pounds, and it must accompany them everywhere—on fourteen-mile runs through soft sand and surf, over rocks, and through barbed-wire obstacles.

The confounded thing must never be seen in a deflated condition: it can never be left unattended, not even for a moment, or it will be deflated by the instructors and must then be inflated with manual pumps before it can be moved. The trainees carry it and swim with it, and occasionally get the luxury of using it for the purpose it was intended. Then they must paddle it faster than some craft move with engines, but it is still a luxury.

And so it continues, week after week, from five o'clock in the morning, sometimes earlier, until long past sunset: swimming, running, obstacle courses, exercises, marching drills, and occasionally some classroom work. Throughout all this, personal hygiene has to be maintained, and clothes, personal effects, and living quarters have to be maintained in spotless condition. There is no spare time.

The end of the first phase of training is highlighted by "Motivation Week," otherwise known as "Hell Week." This week is just one long, almost impossible, round of physical endeavor, feats of endurance, and tests. It culminates in a mock amphibious landing where the trainees must run and crawl in mud and sand for hours on end through simulated shell fire, detonating mines, hand grenades, and machine-gun fire.

All the volunteers think they can take the stress of being under fire in battle—after all, they have lived it in their minds or seen it in the movies again and again. But when they are actually subjected to it, even in training with the knowledge that the charges are set off by their instructors, they are made acutely aware that a mistake can occur that might prove fatal.

Present-day environmentalists have coined the phrase "noise pollution," and the medical profession agrees that noise produces stress. A warrior entering a battle zone is normally under extreme physical and mental stress to begin with, and when he is subjected to the ear-shattering sounds of explosives being detonated around him, the tension and stress levels become almost unbearable.

The tremendous noise causes one type of stress, but the explosions create shock waves that slam into a human body in a most uncomfortable way—and the closer the explosion the worse the feeling. A high-pitched tone starts up in a man's head, and if he tries to talk, it produces a peculiar and uncomfortable feeling. Equilibrium is disturbed so much that walking, and even crawling, straight is difficult and takes a conscious effort. Feeling like retching, being sick, getting terrible headaches, experiencing moments of acute shortness of breath, and watering of the eyes that almost makes it impossible to see, all occur at once. Dirt, sand, mud, and all manner of debris fill the air, along with the acrid smell of the spent explosives.

Trying to think and follow orders under such conditions, even for a brief period of time, is difficult, but it has to be done. Add to that the possibility of incapacitation or death: the resulting feeling, if it has never been experienced before, is horrible.

It is precisely these sensations that the SEAL training is designed to produce, and that is why the volunteers are subjected to it for an extended period of time during that day in hell week. During this one period alone, the largest number of volunteers either quit or are removed from the course because it is discovered that they have something that resembles a fear of explosives.

By the time hell week is over, the class is traditionally

reduced by a further fifty percent, and the few volunteers that remain are now nicknamed "tadpoles."

The second phase of training starts with the emphasis on academic and diving training. A considerable amount of time is spent in the classroom before the actual diving practice starts as the basic principles of diving include physiology, mathematics, physics, some chemistry, hydrography, underwater navigation, underwater communications, diving medicine, a knowledge of certain gases and their properties, and mechanics.

The SEALs use underwater breathing equipment that ranges from the traditional air-breathing rig used by sport divers, commonly called SCUBA (Self-Contained Underwater Breathing Apparatus), to the more complex mixed-gas equipment used by commercial divers, including some very specialized Navy diving equipment. Consequently, they must be totally familiar with the operation and function of all such equipment, and that alone takes up a lot of classroom time.

From the classroom they go to the training tanks, which are really just very deep swimming pools. From the tanks they go to the ocean, and then to freshwater lakes and rivers. Even during the practical training the academic work does not stop. Trainees who do not have adequate academic backgrounds, or who are having academic problems, are sent to nearby civilian colleges for further education. At this stage of training the instructors will make every attempt to assist by giving extra instruction if it is felt that an individual will respond. Loosing a volunteer who has all the physical, disciplinary, attitudinal, practical, and most of the academic qualities is not something the SEALs will accept if a little extra instruction will correct the situation.

By the time the diving training finishes, some seventeen weeks of the course have been used up, and the hard physical training now continues in conjunction with the academic work.

During the final eight weeks of the course, the physical requirements become progressively harder. The trainees are introduced to the old UDT procedure of being dropped in the water from speeding boats, and then being picked up again by the same speeding craft. This involves timing and coordination of the highest order as the swimmer to be picked up must remain stationary as the boat races toward him. Attached to the side of the high-speed boat is an inflatable boat, and kneeling down inside it is a colleague who holds out a ring, or snare. As the coxswain steers the craft past the man in the water, he loops his arm through the snare. Once this happens, the momentum of the speeding boat drags him into the side of the inflatable boat where he quickly rolls inboard and releases the snare to allow the boatman to set up for the next swimmer. When the trainees have learned this method, they are then taught other more recently developed methods that accomplish the same thing; however, the old method is still used for special tasks and must be taught.

There is extensive training in navigation, infantry and commando techniques (such as basic reconnaissance patrolling), ambush techniques, river and stream crossing, rappeling from cliffs and helicopters onto land and into water, sentry disposal, and unarmed combat. There is a weapons course where the trainees are taught to strip, assemble, and operate effectively all infantry weapons currently in use with the United States Armed Forces.

Explosives training is a significant part of this phase of training, and a great deal of emphasis is placed on it. Hand in hand with the explosive training is booby-trap training, with emphasis on learning how to avoid or disarm the fiendish devices.

The final phase of the twenty-five-week training course commences with a comprehensive land and sea reconnaissance conducted under simulated, but extremely dangerous, combat conditions. The reconnaissance exercise is followed immediately by a full-scale SEAL raid on a land installation on a remote island, where the installation is actually destroyed.

This raid is then followed with a full series of underwater demolition raids where complex underwater obstacles have to be blasted away along miles of beaches. Some of the obstacles are set deep enough to afford concealment for the trainees, but most are set in raging surf with the usual barrage of explosives to simulate enemy fire.

At the end of the course there is graduation, when the tadpoles become SEALs—but they only become SEAL "pups," because a considerable amount of training is yet to come. This further training starts when graduation leave is over. At this point the men have the sea and land elements to their credit, but not the air element.

After their leave, the newly appointed SEALs report to the Army Parachute School at Fort Benning, Georgia, for standard airborne infantry-type parachuting, called static line parachuting.

Later, when they are assigned to a SEAL team, they will learn free-fall parachuting from both high and low altitudes, and from a variety of fixed-wing aircraft and helicopters. They will also learn how to parachute while fully equipped in self-contained combat diving equipment, again from a variety of aircraft.

Apart from maintaining their physical condition, the SEALs must now improve their skills with a variety of operational tasks during fleet and other military exercises. They must also learn how to work from submarines and surface ships of the Navy, and how to work with other branches of the armed forces, including the NATO forces.

They must learn at least one foreign language, advanced communications, foreign forces equipment and weapons identification, intelligence procedures, espionage and counterespionage methods, guerilla tactics, jungle operations, desert operations, Arctic and Antarctic operations, skiing, flying (both fixed and rotor wing), military vehicle operation (including tanks), and a host of other skills.

Members of the SEAL teams never stop learning, either during or between operational missions. The training and learning process continues until the day comes when a man must leave the SEALs, perhaps when he is at his peak of usefulness, and that is sad day for the SEALs. However, there is one consolation—there are more volunteers already going through Hell Week!

6

"FATHER OF THE DEMOLITIONEERS"

Draper Kauffman entered the U.S. Naval Academy with the intention of following in his father's footsteps. Understandably, Vice Admiral James Kauffman was pleased that his son had decided to pursue a naval career, but both men were to be disappointed when it was discovered that the younger Kauffman's eyesight was deteriorating.

Despite his high level of achievement at the academy, Draper was not commissioned upon graduating as his eyesight had fallen to 15/20. The Navy of the thirties was quite strict concerning such matters, and no amount of persuasion could move those in command to make an exception. Draper took the eyesight test again, some two years after he had graduated, but there had been no significant change, either in his eyesight or in the Navy's attitude regarding entry requirements.

But Draper Kauffman was not to be denied a career at sea, and he achieved it with the Mercantile Marine by joining the shipping company, U.S. Lines.

THE SEALS:
Sea, Air, and Land

Sea: An Underwater Demolition Team trainee sets a charge on the reefs near Pineros Island, Puerto Rico.

Air: SEALs rappel from a Navy "Seawolf" helicopter. This technique is essential in jungles or wooded areas where parachutes are easily entangled.

Land: In Vietnam, a SEAL team member moves cautiously in the thick wooded area along a stream.

A group of SEALs, camouflaged for stealth, practices an amphibious assault at Salton Sea, California.

Before and after Underwater Demolition Team members leap into the mud during training in Coronado, California.

An Underwater Demolition Team member grimaces with fatigue and strain as he makes his way through a timed obstacle course.

An Underwater Demolition Team practices "drops" from a small inflatable boat at 35 knots.

Underwater Demolition Team recruits strain to hoist a telephone pole during an exercise period at the Naval Amphibious Base in Coronado, California.

U.S. Navy SEALs ready for a mission in Vietnam in 1970.

In September, 1939, when war was declared in Europe, Draper determined that he was not going to sit back and watch. He, like many other Americans, traveled to France and volunteered for service with the French Army. He was accepted for service in the American Volunteers Ambulance Corps and became an ambulance driver. In that capacity he became well know on the front line, as he would take considerable risks to rescue wounded men. On one particular occasion he completely ignored all warnings and proceeded to rescue wounded men in the middle of a fierce firefight. Under heavy machine-gun fire, and with the possibility of a mustard gas attack, he continued to pick up wounded soldiers who lay dying between the French and German front lines. For his actions he was awarded one of the highest French military honors for bravery in battle, the Croix de Guerre.

Unfortunately, the French could not hold back the Nazi stormtroopers, despite assistance from the British, and the main French defense system, the fortress complex called the Maginot Line, collapsed. The well-trained German soldiers easily overran the French Army, and Draper Kauffman was captured and interned in the Lunéville prisoner-of-war camp.

He had not resigned himself to spending the war in prison. Thoughts of escaping were always there, but he did not have to put them into action. The German high command was still attempting to remain on friendly terms with the United States, and it seized every opportunity to demonstrate its good will and best intentions.

In a propaganda statement, the Germans claimed that because the members of the American Volunteers Ambulance Corps and other similar nonaggressive organizations had not taken up arms against the German nation, there had actually been no violation of neutrality. Based on that statement, they released a handful of American ambulance drivers in September 1940 and sent them to England. Draper Kauffman was among them.

By the time Kauffman arrived in England, he had already made the decision that he would attempt to join a fighting force, and naturally he approached the Royal Navy.

To the British, an American trying to join their navy had to be something of a romantic, or in their words "a bit of a cowboy." Despite the fact that they were desperately short of men, the royal Navy did not give in to the requests of friendly foreigners—particularly those who were seeking a commission, and whose eyesight did not meet their requirements. But Draper Kauffman received a commission as a sublieutenant in the Royal Navy for two reasons: one was that he had excellent academic qualifications, and the other, which was more important, was that he volunteered for mine disposal.

To the members of the Royal Navy selection board, any educated "fool" who volunteered for mine-disposal duties had to be taken seriously, and 20/20 vision was not considered to be a requirement. Mine-disposal personnel needed steady nerves and hands with a sensitive touch. Since they would have an almost intimate relationship with the articles that could destroy them, they did not have to rely on natural eagle-eyed vision.

The Royal Navy's official name for the unit that Kauffman was assigned to was "Mine Disposal," although it was often referred to by the old name of "Mine Defense Organization."

After a somewhat short course in the techniques of disarming all known enemy bombs and mines, Kauffman was sent to work in London as the city was now being subjected to the blitz.

Any bomb- or mine-disposal expert will tell you that

the bombs you know about are relatively easy to deal with. It is the ones you have never seen before that can cause grief. The Germans were aware of the British bomb- and mine-disposal crews, and as some of the bombs they were dropping were not intended to explode immediately, the German ordnance experts designed booby-trap devices in order to deter the disposal crews. The installation of time-delay mechanisms in the bombs was an attempt by the Germans to terrorize the British people. It was felt that if bombs were suddenly to start exploding long after the bombers had left the area, it would create an adverse psychological effect. The Germans were correct in their thinking, but they underestimated the courage and ingenuity of the disposal crews, as well as the resolute strength of the citizens of London.

Mines were normally dropped by parachute, so that they would not explode on impact when they landed in the water. Soluble "pins" were used so that the parachutes would detach after a few moments of immersion, and the mine would then float just below the water's surface to await detonation by the first vessel to strike it. Dropping floating mines in rivers was quite effective, as they would move with the current and collide with stationary vessels or loading docks and detonate. Some of the mines did not require an impact to detonate them, they had magnetic and acoustic detonators that only required the sound or the steel mass of a passing vessel to set them off. All mines were assumed to have magnetic and acoustic detonators, and consequently the disposal crews had to use nonmagnetic tools. Moreover, they could not create excessive noise. Like the bombs, mines were also rigged with complicated booby-trap devices to deter the disposal crews.

The port of London, on the river Thames, was an ideal target for the German mine-laying aircraft, but more often than not, the mines would be carried with the wind and fall on the city. They then had to be dealt with by the Navy mine-disposal crews. Traditionally, the Army bomb-disposal crews dealt with the bombs and the Navy with the mines; but because of a shortage of Army bomb disposal experts and because more bombs than mines were dropped on London, the Navy men were cross-trained to assist the overworked Army men.

During his first few months in mine disposal, Sub-lieutenant Kauffman was kept quite busy. The Germans commenced a heavy mining program around the London docks, and, in the eyes of his colleagues and superior officers, it was felt that Kauffman was an "old hand" and stood every chance of surviving in the profession. The reason for their optimism was that he was still alive after six weeks of work, and it was during that period that most new bomb- and mine-disposal officers were killed.

On one occasion, just before Christmas 1940, old hand Kauffman experienced his first "runaway." He received a call from his commanding officer ordering him to gather his crew and take them with him to dispose of a large mine that had fallen into a residence. When he arrived at the street address, the police had already evacuated the occupants of the house and all the nearby residents; they had also barricaded the street to prevent traffic from entering.

As Kauffman was going through the barricade, a police sergeant informed him, with a slight cough, that the mine was located in the "gentleman's sitting room," in what was politely called a "house of ill repute." Kauffman found the mine in the gentleman's sitting room— it had come through the roof of the building, crashed through one room and then down into the sitting room. The two-thousand-pound monster had come through the ceiling and had imbedded itself in the floor. Its parachute was still attached, and the canopy was neatly entangled in the massive chandelier that was hanging at a crazy angle from the ceiling. The room was adorned with Christmas decorations, some of which had been pulled down and were now mockingly strewn over the one-ton mine.

After examining the monster, he went back to get his tools and equipment and to explain to his colleagues and crew the location and position of the weapon and how he proposed to deal with it. He returned to the gentleman's sitting room and set to work to disarm the mine. As he was carefully working on the fuse guard, a whirring sound suddenly started up from within the mine case. Kauffman was seen running out the front door of the house at an unbelievable speed. His waiting crew instantly took cover and held their hands over their ears. He had covered some forty yards when the mine went off, completely demolishing the house and the adjoining buildings. Other houses in the area were severely damaged by both the blast and the flying debris.

Kauffman was caught in the blast and hurled through the air. When the dust and rubble settled down, his colleagues found him, battered and bruised, but alive. He was taken to the hospital where it was discovered that his worst injury was internal, in the form of a damaged kidney.

The official report, written by Captian C. N. E. Curry, R. N., noted that, "this would indicate that Sublieutenant Kauffman did the equivalent of one hundred yards in eight seconds; it is possible that his extreme sense of urgency enabled him to do so."

It was a rule in the Royal Navy mine-disposal service that once a man had a bomb or mine explode on him, assuming of course that he lived, he would immediately be removed from the disposal teams. Kauffman had been informed that he would not be allowed back in disposal, and he was extremely unhappy about it. However, while he was still recovering from his injuries, a mine landed on a nearby airfield, and the nearest officer with experience in that type of mine, apart from Kauffman himself, could not get there for at least eight hours. Kauffman telephoned his superiors and persuaded them to let him disarm the mine.

It was with considerable nervousness and controlled fear that he approached the mine, but he safely removed the fuse and disarmed the mine to everyone's relief—mostly his own.

The Royal Navy allowed an exception to its rule, and Kauffman was allowed back in the disposal teams, where he continued to work long, nerve-straining hours disarming a variety of mines and bombs that the Germans dropped on the embattled island.

In November, 1940, Kauffman was given permission to take his well-earned leave back in the United States. While in Washington, he was approached by Rear Admiral William Blandy who was Chief of the Bureau of Ordnance. Blandy was a friend of Kauffman's father and had heard some of the stories concerning the younger Kauffman. He asked Kauffman if he would return to the States and establish a U.S. Navy bomb-disposal unit. The Navy was prepared to forego their eyesight requirement to obtain an explosives expert, and Kauffman would be commissioned as a lieutenant commander in the U.S. Naval Reserve.

He readily agreed to the admiral's proposal, and an unusual transfer was arranged from the British Royal Navy to the United States Navy.

A month had not passed when the Japanese attacked Pearl Harbor, and the newly commissioned Kauffman was flown to Hawaii to help with the disposal of the unexploded Japanese bombs in the aftermath of the deadly raid. He found that the Japanese bombs were extremely unsophisticated compared to the German bombs, and, having spent a year working with some of the most deadly bombs and trick-fuse mechanisms in the world, he had little difficulty in disarming the Japanese ordnance. Those who worked with him in and around Pearl Harbor were suitably impressed with his knowledge, ability, and unshakeable nerve.

When no further unexploded bombs could be found in Hawaii, Kauffman set about the task that Admiral Blandy had assigned him, and for the next seventeen months he organized and ran the Bomb Disposal School.

At the beginning of May, 1943, Draper Kauffman got married and was in the middle of his honeymoon when he received a telegram ordering him to report to Washington at once. The telegram is reputed to have arrived late in the afternoon, and Kauffman, it appears, instructed the messenger boy to bring it back the following morning.

When he reported to Washington, he was instructed to gather some men together and train them to destroy any form of beach obstacle that the enemy, either German, Italian, or Japanese, might decide to place on its beaches to hinder Allied amphibious assault landings. He was also informed that he could locate his training school anywhere he chose, and that he could recruit men, in or out of the navy, and order equipment from wherever he wished. Finally, he was told that it was an emergency, and that he must start immediately.

Kauffman set to work with his usual enthusiasm, and the Naval Combat Demolition Units had their first official home in Fort Pierce, Florida.

By the beginning of 1944, the training school at Fort Pierce was running smoothly and efficiently. Most of the graduates were being assigned to Admiral Turner's newly formed Underwater Demolition Teams headquartered in Hawaii. Kauffman felt he had done his job and wanted to get back into action again, but all his requests for transfer to an active team were denied on the grounds that he was needed at Fort Pierce to continue training the men for demolition teams in both the Atlantic and the Pacific.

Draper Kauffman did not stop trying, and on one occasion he was called to Washington to explain to his superiors how and why they had received two identical signals within the same week from two different admirals—Turner in Pearl Harbor and Alan Kirk in London. The signals requested that Lieutenant Commander Kauffman be transferred to their commands immediately.

Kauffman received a resounding "telling off" and was sent back to his command at Fort Pierce. However, he kept trying. He sent a request to Admiral Turner begging him to use his influence and have a transfer effected. The admiral had heard plenty about Kauffman, although he had never met him, and in April, 1944, Kauffman was ordered to report to Maui, Hawaii, to take command of Underwater Demolition Team Five in preparation for the invasion of Saipan.

At Saipan, Admiral Turner decided to test Kauffman with a new idea, and the result was an Underwater Demolition Team conducting its reconnaissance and demolition raids in broad daylight and within yards of the enemy positions. It was made possible by a tremendous bombardment screen, under which the UDT worked, that was put up and maintained by Admiral Turner's battleships.

The success of the operation brought about a significant change in UDT tactics. Instead of working at night, using only darkness and stealth for protection and having to make do with whatever information it could get, the UDT could virtually take its time and conduct very detailed reconnaissance missions and perform extensive demolition work.

Draper Kauffman remained in the Pacific Theater for the rest of World War II. He was promoted to commander and had to relinquish Team Five when he was appointed to the position of Chief of Staff, UDT Pacific.

Throughout his time in the Pacific, he was continually devising new methods, tactics, and techniques for UDT operations. He was responsible for most of the operational planning for the UDT up until the Japanese capitulated, and he was one of the first Navy officers to set foot in Japan.

When the war ended, he was sent to Coronado, California, to establish a permanent UDT training school, and he was promoted to captain with a commission in the regular Navy.

Draper Kauffman remained with the Navy and, like his father, achieved the rank of vice admiral. He is probably best remembered as "Father of the Demolitioneers," a name given to him in honor of his efforts, endeavors, and tremendous enthusiasm during his service in World War II.

7

STINGRAYS

The disastrous amphibious assault on the Japanese-held island of Tarawa during World War II produced an urgent demand for new methods of beach reconnaissance and the destruction of underwater obstacles. This demand, coming from the highest authority in the Navy, not only brought about the formation of the one-hundred-man Underwater Demolition Teams, it also brought about the invention of various mechanical contrivances that were designed solely for the purpose of clearing underwater obstacles.

One such piece of equipment was given the somewhat ambiguous name of "Reddy Fox." This was a giant tube filled with explosives, and attached to the rear end was a conventional torpedo. This huge, glorified torpedo was intended to be aimed in the direction of any offending reef or obstruction and then set off. When it hit the reef, it would explode, and, because of the size of the charge that was packed inside the device, it was supposed to blow open a considerable gap. It seemed like a reasonable idea, but during testing it was found that it was almost impossible to get the devices to maintain a constant depth beneath the surface in anything but perfectly calm water. They would often porpoise out of the water and then dive back in, going straight to the bottom where they would promptly explode. Occasionally, they would find a small obstruction on the way to the reef and again detonate prematurely.

Those that did manage to get to the reef would sometimes be deflected upward causing them to leap over the reef and either explode on the other side, stick on the reef itself, or head straight for the beach and become stranded. Finally, when they actually did what they were supposed to do—that is, hit the reef and explode—they simply did not open a large enough gap. As a result of the control problems and the lack of effective reef destruction, the "Reddy Fox" was dropped.

Another invention was the "Woofus" boat, which was just a landing craft loaded with rockets that were aimed down at the reefs. It, too, proved unsuccessful in blowing gaps, although it was quite spectacular to watch in operation.

The secret weapons that seemed to offer the most chance for success were the "stingrays." These were ordinary landing craft filled with tons of high explosives that were scuttled to sink on top of the reefs or obstacles. Once in position, they were detonated, and the massive charges would blow a considerable gap in any reef or man-made defense barrier. The most significant factor was that they were remotely operated by radio control, thereby eliminating the necessity for men to risk their lives getting them into position.

The first stingrays were supplied to the newly formed Underwater Demolition Team Numbers One and Two at their headquarters and training base in Hawaii. Captain Edward Brewster was in command of Team One and under him, in temporary command of Team Two, was Lieutenant Thomas Crist. It became Crist's responsibility to learn the operating principle of the stingrays and to teach the men from both teams how to use them in preparation for the upcoming invasion of Kwajalein Atoll in the Pacific.

The Underwater Demolition Teams were intrigued with the idea and set about the task of perfecting their skills in operating the craft. There were four primary controls on the vessels: steering, engine operation, scuttling, and detonation. The men spent days learning how to operate and contol the drones from a specially equipped landing craft called the command vessel. The most difficult part of the operation was learning how to steer the drones when they were coming straight toward the command vessel: the controls had to be used in the opposite sense—steer left to go right, and vice versa. "Backward thinking," was what it was known as among the men, and it took quite a bit of practice to do it automatically.

The team worked out an operational sequence for using the boats where the drones were manually operated up to the line of departure. The crews of the explosive-laden stingrays would set the controls as they approached the departure line and then throw an inflatable boat over the side. They would take one last look to ensure that everything was working, and then cast off to wait for the command vessel following the drone to pick them up. The "operator" would take control of the stingray when its crew signaled that they had set it on remote, and he would continue to guide the explosive-laden robot toward the target area.

The coxswain of the command vessel would pay no attention to the drones; he would keep his craft moving at a steady speed and exactly on the plotted course. This avoided the hilarious situations that had developed during training when both the drone coxswain and the command craft coxswain, who were standing a few feet away from each other, both tried to keep up with one another. It was quickly discovered that the command craft coxswain must pay no attention to what the drone was doing; he must just steer in the correct direction and leave the stingray operator to control both the separation distance between the two vessels and the drones' direction.

Lieutenant Crist informed Admiral Turner's Operational Readiness Officer, Captain Tom Hill, that his team was ready for action with the stingrays. The captain requested that Crist set up a live explosive demonstration, using just one stingray, for the admiral and his staff.

Meanwhile, an operational modification was being carried out on one of the drones, something that invariably happens when a new piece of equipment is put into service, because there is always someone who is not quite satisfied with it the way it is. That someone was a member of Team Two who felt it was a perfect waste to send hundreds of stingrays to their doom, when they were so close to the enemy, without at least using them to get a shot at the enemy.

It was decided that the ideal weapon was the tube-type, multiple-launch rocket system that was used by the preinvasion bombardment vessels. Everyone seemed to agree that the sight of the stingrays steaming toward the shore, momentarily stopping over the reef to release a barrage of rockets, then immediately submerging and exploding on the reef, would utterly confuse and bewilder the Japanese.

Crist signed the procurement request, and shortly afterward the rocket system was made available. The supply officers never questioned the often strange requests from the UDT, basically because the teams' function was classed as secret and a directive had been put out by Admiral Turner that they were to be issued anything requested.

The rocket system was installed on the drone that was to be used in the demonstration for the admiral and his staff, and it was connected to one of the spare radio control functions. Commander Brewster shook his head in wonder when he saw the armed stingray—although he knew it was being built, he had not seen it until just prior to the demonstration. However, Admiral Turner's staff and invited guests seemed to be rather impressed.

A small island off the coast of Hawaii was used as a target, and the demonstration commenced with Crist displaying the maneuverability of the drone by putting it through a series of turns ahead of the command vessel. At the conclusion of this demonstration, the stingray was sent toward the beach until it reached the buoys that marked the imaginary reef. Crist operated the controls for the rocket launchers, and moments later long stabbing fingers of flame were seen coming from the launch tubes. This was followed by a great whistling and snorting sound as the rockets left the tubes and roared toward the tiny island where they landed and exploded.

However, one of those strange situations, usually caused by lack of foresight, developed. The mass of flame produced by the departing rockets set the cargo of explosives on fire. Commander Brewster suggested that the charge be fired before the explosives and the boat burned up completely, but Lieutenant Crist pointed out that the fire would set the charge off as soon as it reached one of the detonating fuses. He had just finished the sentence when the three tons of TNT exploded in the stingray, and the array of debris, flame, smoke, and water that was hurled in the air thoroughly impressed all the observers, including the members of the Underwater Demolition Teams.

There were three positive results from the demonstration. The first was that it demonstrated that Crist and his men could operate the vessels, and that the stingrays would definitely explode. The second was that the rocket launchers should not be used, regardless of their spectacular effect and the somewhat doubtful demoralizing effect they would have on the enemy. The third was that the massive explosion killed hundreds of large tuna fish that the team members collected and transported to shore. None of the fish were eaten by the men; instead, they were exchanged for a couple of cases of imported whiskey—"imported," that is, from the mainland.

The whiskey from the mainland must have been a good omen, because shortly after the demonstration—just before Christmas 1943—UDT Two was ordered to San Diego to join Rear Admiral Richard Conolly's Fifth Amphibious.

UDT One went with Admiral Turner's fleet to Kwajalein, the largest atoll in the world, and it was here that Admiral Turner decided to put the stingrays through their first test under actual battle conditions. Turner was well aware of the fact that he did not need the services of the stingrays, as the reefs off Kwajalein were known to be small and would present no difficulty for the landing craft and amphibious tractors. He did, however, need a conclusive test in order to assess the future use of the vessels, and Kwajalein seemed like an ideal opportunity.

To the west of the main island of Kwajalein is the tiny island of Enubuj, and it was on the reef around this island, over which the assault landing craft would easily pass on their way to the main island, that the stingrays were to be tested. Just before dawn on January 31, 1944, the preinvasion bombardment of the island commenced, and, as the first salvo was falling on the island, Underwater Demolition Team One went into action with its robot boats.

Two of the drones, manned by temporary human crews, were dispatched toward the beach with one command vessel, from which both drones would be controlled, following a short distance behind. The first command vessel was followed by another command vessel and one spare stingray—which would be used in the event of a failure in the first three boats.

When the first two drones reached their appointed line of departure, the crews set them on remote, confirmed that the command vessel had control of them, and then climbed into their inflatable boats and cast off.

Despite the fact that the sea was very choppy, everything seemed to be working out as planned. The first problem came when the drones were within about six hundred yards of the reef. One of the stingrays started to slow down and would not respond to a signal for an increase in power. The command vessel crew members watched in amazement as they saw the reason for the slow down—the drone was going under, just like a submarine. They were still staring at one another in disbelief when the second stingray, as if in sympathy with the first one, stopped moving and started to wallow in the choppy sea.

At this point the second boat sent the spare drone into action. Moments after the temporary crew had left it, the engine stopped and it too started to wallow around. The crews paddled their inflatable boats back toward both stingrays and frantically tried to start the engines. Their efforts were in vain, as their alotted time ran out, and they saw the first waves of Marine-laden assault craft heading toward them. The drones were quickly taken under tow by the command vessels and pulled clear of the advancing assault craft.

The test was a total failure, and the disappointed crews of the command vessels towed the defunct stingrays back to their transport ship to conduct an investigation.

Admiral Turner conducted his own investigation and discovered that supply officers had provided old and worn-out landing craft to be used as stingrays. Since the boats were going to be destroyed in action, and as they did not believe the operation stood any chance of success, they did not feel that they should sacrifice good boats. Admiral Turner, of course, had the last word with the offending officers, who, he said, had acted "inexcusably and without the knowledge of the Force Commander [himself]."

As a result of the investigation, the stingray plan was not scrapped, and another test was planned. This time it was to be held in Europe, in the Mediterranean, during the invasion of southern France.

The Underwater Demolition Team gathered at Salerno, Italy, to prepare for the invasion, both for the demolition of beach defenses and for the operational tests of the stingrays (now sometimes called "Apex" boats).

The fitting and testing of the stingrays was to take place in and around Salerno harbor. Scores of drones were available, all in good condition, and the installation crews, engineers, and radio control technicians were flown in from the States to work on them.

As the beach defenses off the coast of France were almost all man-made concrete and steel structures, which were not as easily removed as natural coral reefs, a new operational plan had to be devised. This plan called for two different sizes of drones to be used; the smaller ones—called "males"—would each carry a ton of high explosives, and they would be sent in first to blow small gaps in the defenses. Once the males were detonated, larger drones—called "females"—each filled with four tons of high explosives, would be sent in to widen the gaps. A maximum of three males would be controlled from each command boat, and a maximum of two females would be controlled from separate command boats.

The landings on the French coast were to take place between the towns of Cannes and Toulon.

To the left, or west flank, were the most heavily protected beaches, with rows of large concrete tetrahedrons capped with mines. The beach assault planners decided that in this area the largest concentration of drones would be used: six males and eighteen females. The Underwater Demolition Team was informed that it must practice with a flotilla of this size, without actually being told where the landings were to take place. The team was given a beach area just outside Salerno to practice on, and it trained by running the empty drones right up onto the beach. Security, it seems, was somewhat lacking, and despite questions that the team officers put to superiors about such visibility concerning a supposedly secret operation, they were simply told to do as they were ordered. The men need not have worried about security, as the Germans already knew the exact time, date, and the very beaches where the landings would take place.

The trial runs with the stingrays were carried out without too many problems. Senior members of the invasion planning staff were on hand to observe the robotic craft in action and to confirm that they were working as they were supposed to. However, the planners were taking no chances, and they instructed that all members of the UDT who were not actually involved with the operation of the drones be held in reserve behind the waves of stingrays in preparation for their more traditional roles: placing charges by hand.

With the training period at an end, the drones were prepared for the invasion and loaded with their explosives. The members of the team who were to follow in reserve behind the drones prepared their Hagensen packs, waterproof detonators, primacord fuses, and inflatable boats.

August 15, 1944, was D-day, and by 0300 hours the invasion fleet was in position off the coast of France. As dawn revealed a bright sky with a few clouds, the aerial bombing and naval shelling began. At the same time waves of drones headed for the beaches—they had but two hours to open up the beach defenses for the assault landing craft.

On the left flank, in front of Cavalaire Bay, six male drones and their command vessels led the way. They were followed closely by eighteen female drones and their control vessels. All six males appeared to detonate in their assigned positions, and the full wave of eighteen females was released. Fifteen of them exploded close to their assigned areas, and from the size of the water spouts and the amount of debris that was hurled in all directions, it appeared they had done their job.

Two of the females just stopped and could not be fired remotely. An escorting submarine chaser was asked to shell them until they did explode.

The last female drone went beserk. It appeared to go to full throttle and then started to charge around in all directions. All attempts to detonate it failed, and they had to be stopped as the vessel approached assault wave guide boats and escorts. The gunners on the other vessels tried to get a clear shot at it; some were not so careful about where they were shooting, and things were starting to get nasty. The beserk drone finally singled out the submarine chaser that was trying to maneuver carefully away, and charged in its direction. The captain of the chaser moved his craft smartly out of the way, but the fiendish drone exploded as it was going past and severely damaged the chaser, putting it out of action for the remainder of the invasion.

A quick examination of the area where the fifteen drones had exploded revealed that they had not done their job. The control boats then raced in under heavy fire and commenced the task they were much better at—placing charges accurately by hand and positively blasting the obstacles out of the way.

In the center position of the assault beach the reconnaissance swimmers reported back that there were no underwater obstacles, apart from mines, and the stingrays were signaled to move away as there was nothing for them to do. The fast inshore minesweepers then came in and swept ahead of the assault waves to take care of the mine problem.

On the east flank, a large submarine net blocked the entrance to Agay cove, but there were no other obstacles. Lieutenant Edward Clayton, one of the few regular Navy officers in the Underwater Demolition Teams, led in two small groups at high speed and placed hand charges along the net. They were subjected to a constant hail of small arms fire as they worked, but they completed the task and blew the net to allow the assault craft through.

The landing area in front of the town of St. Raphaël was well defended with the mined concrete and steel tetrahedrons. Behind the beaches, the enemy guns were placed within the heaviest fortifications along the entire landing area. Rear Admiral Spencer Lewis was in charge of this section of the assault, and he ordered the stingrays to be dispatched.

Four male drones led twelve females toward the narrow beach. They were escorted by the famous rocket bombardment ships that were going to provide additional covering fire. As the drones approached the one-thousand-yard line, they were turned on to remote control by the drone crews and handed over to the command vessels. Just before the hand-over occurred, concealed 88-mm guns opened up from the shore and started "walking" a precise pattern of shells toward the drones and the rocket ships. The shelling was just too accurate to permit any further advancement toward the beach, and all the vessels, drones, and escorts alike had to turn away. As they pulled away, they called for more covering fire from the battleships lying offshore.

Meanwhile, hundreds of assault craft laden with troops had to continue going around in circles several miles out at sea; they could not approach the beaches until gaps had been cleared for them. The battleships found the range of the beach within minutes, and the stingrays and rocket ships turned back toward the beaches. The 88-mm shelling started up again, but not with the accuracy it had displayed the first time. The one-thousand-yard line was reached again, and the drone crews set the controls and transferred to the command vessels. The 88s seemed to be getting more accurate again, but it was too late to do anything about it now.

The drones had barely reached the eight-hundred-yard line when things really started to go wrong. The operators on the command vessels found that their drones were not responding to the signals, and the stingrays started to weave around drunkenly. One female did a perfect 180-degree turn and then held a steady course back out to sea toward the waiting assault craft. The respective command vessel raced after it, and two team members leapt aboard as the vessels closed. They disconnected the explosives and brought the drone under manual control.

The operators were frantically trying to get the drones under control, but they just would not respond. Three of the boats had arrived in the vicinity of the target area, and the operators managed to detonate them; but they did not clear a gap. Two drones ended up on the landing beach with their propellers still thrashing wildly in the surf; all attempts to detonate the charges failed. Another female turned back from the beaches and started to head out toward the assault waves, and, again, despite the fact that the charges had been fired, another two UDT members leapt aboard, rendered it safe, and took control. An explosion far out on the left flank was caused by a male, which had taken off at high speed, running aground on the beach.

The remainder of the drones were racing around in circles, zig-zagging, stopping and starting, and generally creating havoc among the rocket boats that either had been brave enough, or foolish enough to stay.

The danger of the crazy drones was one thing, but, as all this was going on, the 88-mm shore guns were finding their range again, and salvos were falling exactly every three minutes. The men in the command boats never thought the day would arrive when they would wish the enemy gunners would get their act together and hit American boats, but that is exactly what they were hoping for. They could not attempt to shoot at the wildly maneuvering drones themselves; it was far too dangerous with all the other vessels around.

Admiral Lewis could make no sense out of the melee: he could not release his assault troops from their holding positions; his own crazy robot boats filled with high explosives were stopping him. His invasion force was simply being repulsed by his own ships.

The admiral could wait no longer. He called off the landings at St. Raphaël and moved his ships some miles farther to the east where he knew there was a beach that had been opened without the use of demolition crews.

As he moved the fleet, the admiral sent a signal to the harried Underwater Demolition Teams, informing them that they could withdraw from the area and leave their beserk drones to the enemy gunners. The team complied with the instruction.

The drones' independent behavior was thought to be caused by a barrage of radio signals sent out by the Germans. Intelligence reports after the invasion clearly showed that the belief was unfounded. The problem really rested in the radio frequencies used in the control system. They were just too close to other frequencies that were being used, and the system itself was prone to picking up interference.

The primary source of interference was created by the multitude of transmissions that were occurring just prior to the assault landings.

Needless to say, the Navy was not very excited about the use of drones for the remainder of the war. If it had not been for a quick-thinking admiral, the Navy would have suffered its first defeat in an amphibious landing.

However, the use of the stingrays was a genuine attempt to eliminate the risks of sending good men into the face of the enemy to perform extremely difficult and dangerous tasks. The Underwater Demolition Teams did their best to make the system work, and their reward is certainly the success of the remote-controlled craft used by the present-day Navy, particularly those remote-control devises used by the SEALs.

8

BATTLEFIELD LOG:
Yap Island—August 18, 1944

The Office of Strategic Services, more usually called
the OSS, was a secret and clandestine organization that became famous for its espionage work. Its primary purpose
was to train agents and saboteurs to work behind the enemy
lines and to supply qualified personnel for the training of
guerilla and resistance groups in enemy-held countries.
Training was just one of their responsibilities. Another, and
perhaps more important responsibility, was to get the
agents into the country they were assigned to.

As a result, the OSS, among other things, became expert in modes of transportation, and it is almost true to say
that it was a completely self-sufficient military organization.
It had its own specially trained air wing, land force, and
maritime group, including all the necessary support personnel and equipment.

Apart from specialized civilians, the OSS could easily
have boasted that it had personnel from every single military organization in the United States and Britain, as well as
a few other Allied nations.

Major General William Donovan was in command of the OSS, and in mid-1944, he was looking for a place to utilize some of his highly trained men. During a secret conference with Admiral Chester Nimitz, Commander in Chief of the Pacific Fleet and the Pacific Ocean Area, Donovan revealed a list of the highly trained groups he was trying to find a use for. Nimitz carefully studied the list and informed Donovan that, among others, he could use the qualified underwater swimmers of the maritime unit.

The OSS Maritime Unit was under the command of Lieutenant Arthur Choate, and the members of his unit were some of the most multitalented individuals in the armed forces. They came from the Navy, Marines, Army, and Coast Guard; some had been recruited into the OSS straight from civilian occupations where they had been employed in a variety of occupations—from professional lifeguard work to deep-sea salvage operations.

As members of the OSS, they were well trained in raiding techniques, demolition, reconnaissance, air, land, and sea sabotage operations, parachuting, weapons, unarmed combat, and numerous other deadly skills. Most of the unit had been trained in the States and had been in action overseas with British units involved in underwater warfare.

Some of Lieutenant Choate's maritime unit were sent to Europe and Southeast Asia at the request of the various area commanders who had special operations groups of their own. However, the majority of the unit—twenty-one enlisted men and five officers, including Choate—were assigned to the Underwater Demolition Teams and sent to the Pacific area training camp at Maui, Hawaii. It is interesting to note that the range of skills, and part of the mission role of the OSS unit, was more or less identical to that of the present-day SEALs.

* * *

At about the time the OSS men were informed of their mission with the Underwater Demolition Teams, Class 6A was completing its training at Fort Pierce, Florida. Part of the class was allocated for the formation of Team Ten, which was commissioned at Fort Pierce shortly after the class graduated. Lieutenant Commander McAdams was appointed to lead the team, and on June 2, 1944, it departed from San Francisco on board the USS *Monterey* for Maui.

When the team arrived in Maui, on June 19, it was joined by the OSS group. Lieutenant Choate became the commanding officer, and Lieutenant Commander McAdams was transferred to other duties.

One of the first actions of Lieutenant Choate and his OSS crew was to teach all the remaining members of Team Ten how to use swim fins. Up until that time every UDT member swam either barefooted or with coral shoes or boondockers. The use of swim fins had been discontinued during early tests conducted at Fort Pierce because they had caused cramps. The OSS men had perfected the technique of using fins and other specialized underwater swimming equipment, and they soon taught their colleagues in Team Ten how to use the fins correctly.

When Commander John Koehler, Commanding Officer of the Underwater Demolition Team training base on Maui, and the other team commanders saw Team Ten in action with the swim fins, they realized that their own experienced swimmers were sadly lacking.

Commander Koehler sent his request for swim fins to the base supply officer almost immediately. No longer surprised by anything that these "half fish, half nuts," as one famous admiral called them, requested, the amused supply officer just purchased every available set of fins in both Hawaii and the United States. He was quite surprised when he was informed that his "clean out of the United States"

was not enough and orders had to be sent out to manufac-
urers to have thousands of new sets made.

Since the Underwater Demolition Team operations
were classified as secret, supply officers were not allowed to
ask the question "What for?"—regardless of how strange a
request might be. A supply officer once became so alarmed
about the "welfare" of the men in the Underwater Demolition Team that he asked to speak with the senior UDT officer. The confidential meeting took place, and the supply
officer stated that he was concerned about the fact that requests from the teams for condoms exceeded ten times the
total garrison strength on the islands of Hawaii. Did he, a sen-
or officer of the UDT, know that his men were sex maniacs?

The Underwater Demolition Team officer answered
the man by taking him to the explosives area to let him
watch several men loading detonators into the prophylactic
devices. The so-called waterproof detonaters were not as
waterproof as they were supposed to be, and because a wet
detonator could jeopardize a complete operation—and had
in the past—the UDT men had reverted to the old soldier's
trick for keeping gun barrels dry: condoms.

As the swim fins arrived from the States, Lieutenant
Choate assigned men to instruct the members of the other
UDT teams in their use—not only for use in the water, but
also in walking on land and scrambling over rough coral and
beaches with them.

Preparations were being made for the invasion of the
islands of Peleliu and Yap, and both aerial and submarine
periscope reconnaissance photographs clearly showed that
the Japanese were building a series of underwater defenses.
Rear Admiral Paulus Powell requested a special reconnaissance mission and suggested the use of a submarine and
Underwater Demolition Team personnel.

A request for volunteers produced five men from Team Ten, which was now more usually referred to as the OSS Team. The five were joined by one of the training base instructors, Chief Howard Roeder, an ex-construction battalion member, who had been one of the first members of the UDT, and five other men who were to act as a support group on the submarine and in the inflatable boats. This group of five was comprised of two officers and three enlisted men from the Amphibious Operating Base at Waipio, Hawaii. The senior officer of the group was Lieutenant Commander C. E. Kirtpatic, and the other officer was Lieutenant M. R. Massey.

Chief Roeder was to lead the five men from the OSS Team in the actual reconnaissance of the enemy beaches and, as Admiral Powell considered the mission to be of the utmost importance, he personally briefed Chief Roeder and wished him luck.

Commander Koehler further briefed the chief and all the men in security regulations. He warned them that if they were captured, the Japanese would make them talk, whether they wanted to or not: apart from some well-publicized, brutal interrogation methods, they also had some sophisticated ones.

If they were captured, they were to tell their interrogators that Underwater Demolition Team tactics had changed and that all future beach reconnaissance operations were being conducted from submarines.

The submarine *Burrfish*, a veteran of many patrols, was assigned for the mission. The captain and crew were experienced at close inshore periscope reconnaissance work, and they had also been on numerous patrols where they landed and retrieved guerillas and agents (usually called infiltration and exfiltration missions).

* * *

The *Burrfish* slipped from its sheltered berth in Pearl Harbor on the morning of July 9, 1944, and slowly worked its way through the array of boom defenses into the open sea. The undersea hunter cruised on the surface at a steady seventeen knots for three days and nights through "safe" waters. On the morning of the fourth day, diving stations were sounded, and as the air in the floatation tanks was replaced with water, the *Burrfish* slid beneath the waves. The sound of the diesel engines driving the electric generators was replaced by the steady hum of the electric motors, and as the vessel submerged beneath the wave effect zone, the newcomers to the world of the submariners reveled in the stability of the craft. Despite their cramped quarters, the Underwater Demolition Team members felt comfortably at home, which was largely due to the hospitality of the captain and crew of the *Burrfish* who treated them as VIPs.

Every night the boat rose to periscope depth and conducted a sonar, radar, and visual sweep search. If there was no activity in the vicinity, the captain would bring the boat to the surface to recharge the batteries and air the boat.

The reconnaissance team had settled into the submariners routine by the time the vessel reached the general target area at the beginning of August. There was more activity in the control room and on the bridge of the vessel, and as they entered enemy territory, there was a visible change in the attitude of the submarine's crew; they walked more softly and talked in lowered tones.

Shortly after the captain informed the crew that they were within a day of the target area, the submarine's air-conditioning system went out and living conditions changed quite drastically.

The boat's engineers determined that the problem was on the outside of the vessel on one of the sea valves. One of the OSS team members seemed to be very familiar with the submarine's exterior and the operational function of the failed valve. He also seemed to be well acquainted with the vessel's interior and had impressed the crew with his quiet familiarity and almost instinctive knowledge of the "dos and don'ts" in a submarine. When he offered to repair the valve whenever the vessel surfaced, the chief engineer and the captain readily accepted his offer.

After the customary sonar, radar, and periscope sweep the *Burrfish* surfaced at about midnight under the dim light of a half-moon. When the captain, bridge lookouts, and deck-gun crews had taken up their positions, the UDT swimmer climbed out through a deck hatch and went over the side wearing just mask and fins.

He had just climbed back onto the deck grating, having repaired the offending valve, when the radar operator called that he had a contact. Seconds later the sonar operator confirmed twin screws, possibly a destroyer or subchaser, approaching at high speed. As the bridge and decks were cleared, the lookouts picked up the vessel and confirmed the sonar report—it was an enemy subchaser. The Japanese radar had obviously located the *Burrfish* on the surface and had sent the subchaser to investigate. The captain took the submarine down quickly and started to take evasive action. The sonar operator called that the vessel was searching with his sonar, and the crew was ordered to rig for depth charging.

All the men waited to hear the dreaded "ping" of a contact by the enemy hunter's sonar, and they did not have to wait long. It came only minutes after they had submerged, just as the captain was attempting to steer the *Burrfish* away from the islands and into deeper water. It was only faint at first, but it started to get louder just as the captain found enough water beneath the keel to take evasive action. Within minutes he had dodged the enemy sonar sweep, and shortly afterwards, as if out of temper at losing the contact, the enemy started dropping depth charges.

The inexperienced submariners—most of the reconnaissance team—received their first taste of the depth charging as the boat shuddered in the shock wave. They all agreed that they had changed their minds about the idyllic life of a submariner, to the amusement of the crew who politely informed them that they had not been depth-charged—yet! What they were hearing and feeling was the result of depth charges exploding some miles away. That convinced the members of the reconnaissance team that they really did not like the submariner's life after all. However, they were about to be convinced further when another subchaser joined the search, and for the remainder of the night, the enemy sonar found and lost the submarine repeatedly.

The losing was caused by the skill and experience of the captain, but it did not stop the depth charging, which came uncomfortably close, even for the veteran boat crew.

When daylight came so did another menace: aircraft dropping depth charges on instructions from the subchasers. The deadly game of hide-and-seek became even more intense with the addition of the aircraft and continued throughout the day.

As night fell the aircraft left and the *Burrfish* finally managed to get away from the subchasers net of sweeping sonar. As the sound of the chasers faded and died, everyone began to relax; and when the sonar operators shook their heads to indicate that even they could no longer hear their tormentors, smiles started to appear on the faces of the crew. Sweat-soaked brows were wiped, but it was the sweat of tension and nerves as the air-conditioning system had been working throughout!

The captain took the submarine away from the area, and throughout the following day everyone rested. That night the boat was surfaced again, and battery-charging and airing took place until just before dawn. Before the sky started to gray, the *Burrfish* was beneath the waves and heading back to Peleliu.

The island was reached without incident late in the afternoon, and the submarine settled on the bottom to listen for the enemy and wait for darkness. The surface sweep was conducted just before midnight, and when no enemy vessels were seen or heard the *Burrfish* eased gently upward into the troublesome moonlit sky.

Chief Roeder and three of his team were to conduct the first reconnaissance, and Chief Ball of the Amphibious Operations Base team was to man the inflatable boat since he had the most experience in navigation and boat handling. The submarine crew watched in both amazement and amusement as Roeder and his men covered their entire bodies with the traditional camouflage of the UDT: silver-blue grease.

When everything was prepared, the men climbed into the inflatable boat as it sat on the submarine's deck. On a signal from Ball, the captain took the vessel down, and the inflatable boat was left floating on the surface. As the men paddled away, the submarine continued to submerge—it would hold its position underwater and conduct periscope sweeps at set intervals to watch for the returning boat. Remaining on the surface was far too dangerous, as they had discovered a few nights previously.

Chief Ball steered the boat to within two hundred yards of the shore, and the four swimmers slipped into the water. For two hours they swam along the beach in a gridlike pattern, at times within yards of the beach itself. Finally, when they had completely covered the assigned area, they returned to the boat and the waiting Chief Ball.

Ball then demonstrated his navigational skills by steering the boat out into the open sea, to the position where the *Burrfish* was lurking underwater. After a few minutes waiting, the submarine surfaced slowly only a few yards away, to the delight of the shivering swimmers. When the men and the boat were safely inside the submarine, the captain took it down once again and moved slowly away from the island.

Chief Roeder and his crew reported to Lieutenant Commander Kirtpatic that the complete beach area they had covered was heavily defended by a series of wire cribs filled with heavy coconut logs and linked together with steel cables. Before the dawn the report was radioed to Admiral Powell in Pearl Harbor.

On the following night, the *Burrfish* started in again toward the island, but had to break off when radar and sonar picked up another contact that turned out to be one of the subchasers. The chaser came searching with its sonar, but did not locate the *Burrfish* as it quietly slipped away into the deeper waters offshore. The next day the submarine moved in close enough to get periscope photographs of the shoreline, but once again the relentless subchaser appeared on the horizon. It started to become obvious that the Japanese observation aircraft and radar were picking up the *Burrfish*.

For the next two weeks the chasing and dodging continued in a frustrating and nerve-racking battle of wits, with the submarine barely escaping from the subchasers on several occasions. The pattern was almost always the same, day and night. During the day, the submarine would just manage to get some photographs taken when the "terrible two" would come racing over the horizon with their sonar sweeping. The *Burrfish* would slip away and try to approach at night, but the chasers were patrolling the area too tightly to allow the submarine to get close enough for a night reconnaissance by the swimmers.

Finally, the *Burrfish* left the area and set course for the island of Yap. Admiral Powell decided that the initial swimming survey, along with the periscope photographs, had told him what he needed to know: the island was very heavily defended with underwater obstacles. What the admiral did not know—and neither did the intelligence services—was that Peleliu contained far more troops than had been estimated, and that the interior was a natural fortress of honeycombed rock that the enemy would make good use of. The beaches would be cleared and easily taken, but once inland, the First Marine Division alone would suffer over five thousand casualties.

The *Burrfish* located Yap on its radar, and on the first night moved close to the southern shore. This time it was Lieutenant Massey's turn to take the swimmers toward the shore in the inflatable boat. Massey and four men from the OSS team were in the boat, but only three of the team conducted the survey. They soon discovered that the southern side of the island was similar to Peleliu—heavily defended with beach obstacles. They returned to the *Burrfish* and reported what they had found.

As the *Burrfish* submerged, enemy vessels were heard approaching, and another cat-and-mouse game began with the submarine getting something of a "shakedown."

After two days and nights of wandering around and dodging the subchasers, the submarine made its way around to the eastern coast of the island on August 18, and approached within two miles of the beach. Intelligence reports concerning the island indicated that it was heavily garrisoned and fortified, and the captain of the *Burrfish* was aware of this. Two miles off the coast was as close as he dared bring the submarine, and even that was a little too close.

It was Chief Roeder's turn to lead the team. Once again he had Chief Ball as coxswain with one of the other Amphibious Operations Base men as a swimmer, along with UDT members John MacMahon and Robert Black.

When the *Burrfish* surfaced, the men discovered that the wind was blowing quite strongly and the seas were rough, but Chiefs Roeder and Ball were not concerned by this. Paddling the boat would be more work, but otherwise they felt the choppy seas were to their advantage, as far as concealment from the enemy was concerned.

The submarine settled quickly, and the men paddled shoreward until they came within four hundred yards of the beach. At this point they discovered a barrier reef, and it was decided that Chief Ball should keep the boat to seaward of it for fear that the breakers inside the reef would force the boat right up on the beach. Ball anchored the boat, and the four swimmers slipped over the side.

Fifteen minutes later, Ball saw two swimmers coming back over the reef. As they came close to the boat, he could see that one of the men was being assisted; it was the Amphibious Operations Base swimmer, and the man helping him was Robert Black. When they reached the boat, Ball and Black helped the man into it. It turned out that he had become violently ill swimming in the choppy seas and surf. Although he was a strong swimmer, he was not UDT-trained and had never experienced such violent surf before. Returning to the boat was to his credit; trying to carry on would probably have cost him his life.

Black headed back to the beach to join Roeder and MacMahon, and the man he had assisted quickly recovered.

When the prescribed time arrived and the three swimmers did not return, Chief Ball became concerned. He waited a further thirty minutes, and, realizing that something was wrong, he pulled the boat's anchor inboard and started to move along the reef in the direction that he knew the swimmers had taken.

An extensive search of the reef brought no sign of the men. Since the allotted time, as well as the safety margin, had been used up, Chief Ball was forced to return to the submarine. With just two men to paddle the raft against the wind and sea, it took longer than he had expected, but the *Burrfish* was waiting. Ball had hoped the swimmers might have made it back to the submarine, and he was disappointed to find they were not there.

When the raft was safely on board, the captain held the vessel on the surface and went in very close to the reef. For the remainder of the night, he patrolled closely inshore, but there was no sign of Chief Roeder and his men. As dawn came, the *Burrfish* was compelled to submerge and pull away from the island. When it was fully light, the captain brought his submarine back to the island and again came dangerously close to the reef to conduct a periscope search. The search was futile; there was no sign of the swimmers.

By now the submarine's special sensors had picked up the telltale signs that the Japanese radar had located them; it was only a matter of time before the subchasers and the aircraft would appear.

The captain took the submarine out into deeper water and made the decision that the three men must be given up as lost. Their Underwater Demolition Team colleagues pleaded with him to remain for another night to allow them to go ashore in search of them. They were convinced that Roeder and the men would come back to the reef if they were still alive. The captain listened to their reasoning and turned them down—he had already lost three men, the weather was getting worse, and he knew that the Japanese radar had located the *Burrfish*. He was not going to lose another three men and sacrifice the submarine and its entire crew. It was an extremely painful decision to make.

It appears that Roeder, Black, and MacMahon did come back to the beach the following night, because Japanese documents, which were captured a few months later, showed they had been found hiding on the afternoon of the twentieth.

The captured documents included an interrogation report, in which it was discovered that the men had revealed to the enemy exactly what Commander Koehler had ordered.

Roeder, MacMahon, and Black were placed on board a subchaser for transportaton to prison camps in the Philippines, but nothing was heard or seen of them again.

They were posthumously awarded the Silver Star for their actions, as were their colleagues who survived.

9

BATTLEFIELD LOG:
Yōsu, Korea—August 15, 1950

To Vice Admiral Turner Joy, Commander of Naval Forces, Far East, the small seaport town of Yōsu looked like an inviting target. It was not the only target the admiral liked—he had a considerable number of similar targets in mind—but he had to start somewhere.

A short time after he had conceived the idea of conducting amphibious raids on enemy-held territory, he had been presented with a list of suitable targets by his staff. The idea behind such raids was to harass the communist forces by disrupting their supply lines, and, as the majority of major roads and railways in Korea ran along the coastal region, there was good reason to believe that raiding operations would be effective.

Coastal bombardments and aerial bombing of the supply routes had already begun, and moderate success was being reported. However, an accelerated program was necessary, and General Douglas MacArthur, who was Commander in Chief of the Allied Forces in the Far East, had agreed with Admiral Joy that if amphibious raids could be successfully accomplished, they would be of considerable assistance.

The town of Yŏsu was located on the southern coast of Korea, almost forty-five miles behind the existing enemy lines. Reconnaissance photographs showed that there were three bridges and a railway tunnel close to the edge of town, and they were within three hundred yards of the shoreline. Admiral Joy finally selected it as the target for a trial raid, and planning operations began.

Lieutenant George Atcheson was quite surprised when he was ordered to report to General MacArthur's headquarters for a conference with Admiral Joy and Rear Admiral James Doyle. Junior lieutenants are not normally invited to a conference of admirals, and Atcheson showed his respect by being suitably nervous, something he had no control over.

The admirals put him at ease and then surprised him further when they informed him that he was required to lead his small team on an amphibious raid behind the enemy lines. They politely explained that he was the most senior UDT officer available, and that they wanted to start the raid as soon as possible. They did not have the time to wait until a higher ranking officer with the right experience was found and appointed.

Atcheson had been the first UDT man to conduct a beach reconnaissance in the Korean War. He had been leading a ten-man UDT detachment on a routine training exercise in Japan when the war broke out. Within twenty-four hours he and his men were hastily ordered to report for duty in Korea. Three weeks after their arrival, the lieutenant and one of his men were in the water, surveying the beach approaches to the tiny fishing village of Pohang.

As a result of the detailed UDT survey, ten thousand fully equipped combat troops of the U.S. 1st Cavalry Division were safely put ashore on the Pohang beaches on July

18, 1950. They were quickly moved to the front line and had no sooner dug in when the communist forces attacked. On July 20, after some bitter fighting throughout the day, the cavalrymen managed to push the enemy back. It was obvious that the communist forces could easily have overrun what remained of Korea had the division not been in position so quickly. General MacArthur commended the Navy on its selection and rapid survey of the landing beach, and also the speed with which it had transported and disembarked the troops.

Lieutenant Atcheson left the admirals' conference and immediately organized his small team whose members, in the traditional manner, had been speculating. When the lieutenant announced that they were going on a raid, it was difficult to decide whether they were elated at guessing the reason for the conference, or because they were going into action.

The USS *Diachenko*, a fast destroyer/transport, was assigned as the command vessel, and hasty preparations were made. The captain and crew of the *Diachenko* were familiar with UDT operations, and they were just as eager and enthusiastic about going into action against the enemy as were Lieutenant Atcheson and his men.

Shortly after dark on August 5, the *Diachenko's* engines rumbled and shuddered momentarily as the power was applied for full speed. As the engines settled down at their selected power setting, they emitted a rapid pulsing sound that seemed to vibrate a sense of urgency through the deck plates. The bow of the destroyer developed a white phosphorescence "bone between its teeth" as the ship's speed increased dramatically in response to the added power.

As the fast destroyer ploughed its way along the coast, the raiding party's equipment was checked again and again.

The plan of action was repeatedly discussed until Lieutenant Atcheson was certain that everyone fully understood what was going to happen, and what each and every man's part would be. It was a precombat drill, which helped to calm ragged nerves and ensured that all concerned knew their parts.

Shortly after midnight, the *Diachenko* hove to in a blacked out condition just three miles off Yōsu. A landing craft was lowered to the water loaded with the UDT men, their inflatable boat, and almost a ton of explosives. Lieutenant William Thede was in command of the landing craft, and, with assistance from the destroyer's radar operators, he carefully and accurately guided the assault vessel toward the shore.

When he was about six hundred yards from the beach, he brought the vessel to a halt, and Lieutenant Atcheson and his men launched their inflatable boat and loaded it with explosives and weapons.

They left the landing craft and paddled steadily toward the shore. When they were within two hundred yards of the beach, Atcheson stopped the boat and ordered his men to remain in that position as he and Boatswain's Mate Warren Foley slipped into the water. They would swim in and conduct a short reconnaissance; if there were no problems, they would then signal for the boat to be paddled in.

A gentle surf washed the two men up onto the rocky beach, and they carefully crawled a few feet away from the water. They lay motionless for a few minutes, listening and watching for any sound or sight of the enemy. With no evidence of any enemy, they carefully uncovered their waterproofed pistols and several grenades, and moved cautiously across the rough pebble beach. They came to a steep, sloping embankment made from large stone blocks and paused to listen again.

As they started to climb the wall, they noticed that the moon was rising. It was getting quite light, and that hastened the climb. Once on top of the embankment, they made their way quickly to the bridge at the mouth of the tunnel. They could see no enemy pillboxes or gun emplacements, and everything seemed perfect, except for one thing: the moon.

When they turned and looked back to the beach, they became alarmed—they could clearly see their rubber boat some two hundred yards offshore, the landing craft another five hundred yards out, and behind it, the *Diachenko*, nearly three miles away. It was almost a daylight scene.

Atcheson was concerned. He dispatched Foley to race back to the beach, signal the boat to come ashore, and then guide the men with the explosives to the bridge and tunnel mouth.

Foley departed and Atcheson started to examine the bridge for the best place to locate the charges. After a few minutes crawling around underneath the bridge, he had worked out the charge locations and was just starting to climb one of the trestles close to the tunnel mouth when he heard a strange clattering sound. It was coming from the mouth of the tunnel, but it did not sound like a train.

Atcheson was still trying to decide what it was when an old hand-operated railroad cart rolled out of the tunnel. From his position beneath the bridge he could see that it was crowded with enemy soldiers armed with rifles. The cart stopped and the soldiers started looking in the direction of the beach; some of them produced large flashlights that they aimed in the direction of the shoreline.

The men in the rubber boat had seen Foley's signal and were paddling in toward the beach when the lights suddenly appeared. With well-trained reactions, everyone froze momentarily, until they saw Foley wading out toward them and shouting for them to hurry up. They quickly started paddling again, and when they reached the boatswain's mate, he grabbed a Thompson submachine gun and started back across the beach in the direction of the enemy lights. Seaman Austin and Quartermaster's Mate McCormick grabbed their weapons and followed.

Meanwhile, Lieutenant Atcheson was carefully and quietly climbing up the sloping bank behind the enemy patrol. When he reached the top of the bank, he saw the enemy soldiers shining their flashlights down toward the beach, and he could hear them talking excitedly to one another. He pulled the pins out of two grenades and hurled one into the tunnel mouth and one into the midst of the patrol. There were screams of pain and fright as the grenades went off, with the one in the tunnel leaving a resounding echo.

The enemy soldiers, thinking they had been surrounded, started firing in all directions, mostly away from the beach. Atcheson, somewhat pleased with the commotion he had just created, started to work his way carefully along the inland side of the railway embankment, away from the tunnel mouth.

The enemy soldiers were starting to scramble about on the railroad tracks, and the lieutenant kept his pistol poised, ready for immediate use. He could hear a low, moaning sound in the direction of the tunnel, and he assumed it was coming from one of the soldiers who had been caught in the grenade blast. When he thought he was clear of the enemy, he started to move a little more quickly until he saw some movement in front of him and instantly dived down behind the railroad tracks.

Foley had just reached the bottom of the embankment when the grenades went off. He scrambled quickly up to the top and started running in the direction of the tunnel in an effort to assist the lieutenant. He was promptly shot at— by Lieutenant Atcheson, who mistook Foley for a communist soldier. Fortunately, the range was too great, and Atcheson's pistol shot missed; but the enemy soldiers saw Foley about the same time Atcheson fired and opened up with their rifles. He was hit in the hand and the leg, and was knocked over the edge of the embankment.

The thirty-foot fall onto the rocks below was painful, but apart from considerable bruising, Foley suffered no further injuries. He did not know it at the time—and if he had, he probably would not have been very excited about it—but he had just earned himself the painful honor of becoming the first man in the Navy to be wounded in action during the Korean War.

McCormick saw him fall and scrambled over to him. When he had made certain that Foley was in a reasonably safe condition to be moved, he picked him up and carried him back to the boat. Enemy bullets were popping and whining around him as he struggled over the beach, and he expected to get hit at every step. The men at the boat cautiously returned the enemy's fire, not knowing where the lieutenant and Austin were. As McCormick neared the water's edge, some of the men stopped firing and ran forward to assist with the wounded Foley, who was quickly made as comfortable as possible on top of the explosive charges in the bottom of the boat.

McCormick and the others then pulled the boat off the beach and into the water a little way; they held it in the deeper water in readiness for a rapid departure when Austin and the lieutenant returned. The UDT men were very conscious of the fact that their escape vessel was a floating bomb, and all hoped that their two colleagues would get back before an enemy bullet found its way into the explosives. Although the modern explosives were not supposed to detonate readily when hit by small arms fire, it had happened in the past.

Austin was scrambling up the embankment, and the lieutenant was hiding behind the railway lines on the same side as the enemy. As Austin reached the top, a head popped up from the other side of the railroad tracks. Austin could shoot quite well, and the hat on the offending head was promptly blown off. The head and hat belonged to Lieutenant Atcheson, and, fortunately, Austin realized it just as he squeezed the trigger. He barely managed to pull the gun up to avoid hitting his "target."

Lieutenant Thede, in command of the landing craft hovering offshore, saw the shooting begin, and he ordered his crew into action. He guided the boat in to within seventy-five yards of the beach, as Austin and Lieutenant Atcheson raced back to the shoreline. Enemy bullets were ricocheting off the stony beach around their feet, but the men reached the inflatable boat without getting hit.

Lieutenant Thede's landing craft was now receiving continuous rifle fire, and every available weapon on the craft was turned toward the beach. Thede would not permit any of his men to shoot as he had no idea what was going on, except for the fact that it was obvious the UDT men had been discovered.

As the inflatable boat pulled away from the beach, Austin emptied two full magazines from his Thompson gun in the general direction of the rifle fire. Meanwhile, the men were huddled down and straining as they paddled furiously toward the landing craft.

When he thought that the men had paddled far enough out to be in the deeper water, Lieutenant Thede steered his craft between the inflatable boat and the beach. The landing craft then received all the enemy rifle fire, but the more vulnerable rubber boat was now protected.

The gunners in the landing craft had been given the order to shoot back as soon as Thede saw the boat leave the beach. With obvious enthusiasm, they blasted away at the beach area, which seemed to have some effect as the landing craft did not take as many hits as it had initially.

It took only a few moments for the men to get the injured Foley transferred and to clamber into the comparative safety of the bigger craft. With the inflatable boat in tow, still packed with explosives, Thede pulled the landing craft away from the beach and out of range of enemy fire.

The *Diachenko* had been moving into position and was preparing to provide covering fire when Lieutenant Thede radioed that he and his men were on their way back with one wounded man.

The transfer to the destroyer was effected smoothly and efficiently. The landing craft was hoisted on board, and Foley was taken to the ship's small hospital. As the *Diachenko* left the area, a report was transmitted to Admiral Joy.

Although he shared his men's disappointment at the failure of the raid, Admiral Joy was not to be deterred. He intended to organize things a little better, to pay more attention to items such as the moon, and to provide more protection for the men who were to set the demolition charges. Before the *Diachenko* docked, the admiral was already planning the next raid, which was to take place within one week.

10

BATTLEFIELD LOG:
Korea—August, 1950

Admiral Turner Joy had called for more UDT personnel to be assigned to his command before the aborted raid on Yŏsu. He had also requested that a detachment of Marines be specifically assigned for some special operations.

As Lieutenant Atcheson was leading his ten-man team on the Yŏsu raid, the 1st Provisional Marine Brigade was arriving in Korea. On board the same transport ships was a contingent of Underwater Demolition Team One, led by Lieutenant Commander "Kelly" Welch. When he reported to Admiral Joy, Welch was introduced to Major Edward Dupras, USMC. The admiral quickly explained that he wanted them to work together and organize a series of raids against the enemy supply lines. He gave them the details of the Yŏsu raid and then informed them that they must conduct their first operation within a week.

Welch and Dupras did not waste time. They quickly formulated a plan to utilize a forty-one-man raiding party. Twenty-five were to be UDT personnel, and the remaining sixteen were to be Marines.

The Marines were to be the primary security and fighting element. It would be their responsibility to form a perimeter defense around the target area, while the UDT set the charges. In the event that the enemy discovered the raiding party, the Marines were to hold them off until the demolition men had finished their work. If the enemy forces were too strong, then the Marines would be responsible for calling a halt to the operation and would act as rearguard for the retreating UDT.

Another fast destroyer/transport, the USS *Horace A. Bass*, was assigned as the command ship. The UDT and Marines boarded the vessel in the overcrowded port of Pusan on the night of August 10, 1950.

In the early hours of the morning of August 11, the moorings were slipped and the vessel headed up the east coast toward the port of Tanch'ŏn. By midnight August 12, the *Bass* was holding position some three miles off the North Korean coast, a little way south of Tanch'ŏn.

Although it was only 160 miles up the coast, the *Bass*, having engaged in a series of long, diversionary zigs and zags, with occasional stops and circling maneuvers in order to confuse any watching enemy as to its true destination and purpose, had taken a complete day to get there. The vessel had in fact traveled much farther north, but had turned south again as darkness fell on the night of the twelfth. If the enemy had been tracking the vessel, it would probably have assumed that the *Bass* was conducting some sort of coastal patrol and certainly could not have guessed the true purpose of its wanderings.

It was a moonless night and the seas were moderate. The destroyer was rolling gently as the landing craft was lowered into the water loaded with explosives, rubber boats, and spare ammunition for the Marines. The landing craft pulled away quietly from the destroyer and headed toward the shore. Despite its powerful engines, it made very little noise as the exhausts were muffled with extension pipes that ran down into the water.

The first targets were to be two adjacent tunnel mouths and a bridge, located close to the water's edge just outside Tanch'ŏn. The landing craft, under the command of Lieutenant Commander Welch, moved slowly toward the coastline under the guidance of the ship's sensitive radar. When it was about a thousand yards from the beach, seven rubber boats were lowered into the water, and the sixteen Marines and twenty-five UDT men, all with their faces smeared with dark camouflaged grease, scrambled into them.

The rubber boats remained close to one another as they were paddled toward the surf at the water's edge. They came to a halt about fifty yards from the beach as two UDT swimmers slipped into the water to conduct an initial reconnaissance.

As the two men approached the tunnels, they could hear the sound of voices and men moving about. They moved closer and saw an array of shielded lights and shadowy figures moving around under the lights. They counted at least thirty figures before moving quickly and silently back to the water's edge where they signaled the men in rubber boats not to come any closer. The two men swam out to the boats and reported what they had seen.

Based on the reconnaissance report given by the two men, it was decided that it would not be possible to conduct the operation with any hope of success as the raiding party would almost certainly be discovered. When they arrived at the landing craft, they reported the situation to Welch, who completely agreed with the decision; he did not want a firefight on the first mission. In fact, he did not want a fight on any mission—that was not the object of the operation. If his men were accidently discovered setting charges on a target, they would fight their way out. But to start setting charges with the knowledge that they would almost certainly be discovered was not what Welch considered a "calculated risk."

The rubber boats were hauled on board the landing craft, and it returned to the *Bass*. With the landing craft stowed safely on board, the destroyer headed north along the coast toward another possible target.

As before, it was a tunnel entrance that had been selected from aerial reconnaissance photographs; but it was in a more remote area, and there appeared to be no dwellings or military installations nearby.

Just before midnight the demolition party and their Marine guard set out as they had on the previous night. This time the reconnaissance team found no activity and could see no sentries, and they signaled the seven boats to come ashore.

As Major Dupras established the perimeter defense, the UDT men set about their task of blasting the tunnel mouth.

Lieutenant Edwin Smith was leading a group laden with explosive packs toward the mouth of the tunnel. He was very surprised when he came face to face with a North Korean soldier armed with a rifle and bayonet. Before Smith could move, the soldier dropped the rifle and ran off into the darkness. Smith, somewhat relieved, picked up the rifle and received another surprise—his trophy was a wooden rifle with a bayonet crudely lashed to the "barrel." As Smith and his party continued to the tunnel mouth, the enemy soldier was spotted by one of the veteran marine sentries who, obeying orders, used his razor-sharp knife to take care of the problem.

Before the men got to the tunnel, one of the reconnaissance men came running toward them and signaled them to take cover. Everyone sought cover, what little there was around, and lay perfectly motionless waiting to hear what the trouble was. A few minutes later they heard the reason for their concealment, not by word of mouth, but by the unmistakable sound of a train coming out of the tunnel. Those who had been hiding behind the tracks realized that they were not in quite the right place and moved rapidly away.

The locomotive, hauling eleven freight cars behind it, came huffing and puffing out of the tunnel in a cloud of steam. Everyone remained motionless and hidden, despite the fact that the lumbering, slow-moving train was an ideal target. Lieutenant Commander Welch had given strict instructions—trains and a variety of other tempting targets were not to be attacked until the primary objective had been achieved.

When the train had disappeared from sight, the demolition team continued with its task. The men worked hard and fast, and used almost a ton of explosives—a mixture of TNT, tetryl, and C2 with a ring main fuse of primacord— just inside the entrance of the tunnel itself and along the railroad tracks extending from it.

With the charges set, the Marines were withdrawn from their defensive positions, and, along with most of the demolition men, they were sent back to the boats. Major Dupras and two Marines, along with four UDT officers, remained to give covering fire. With the rest of the men safely back at the boats, the two fuse pullers, Lieutenants Atcheson and Wilson, set the time-delay detonators, and everyone then took off for the boats as fast as he could.

The men reached the boats, which were being held just off the beach in preparation for a hasty departure, and everyone paddled furiously in order to get as far out from the beach as possible.

Major Dupras was looking at Lieutenant Atcheson who was checking the fuse time. The lieutenant had barely nodded his head when a rippling cracking sound, accompanied by a brilliant flash, came from the tunnel mouth. Everyone stopped paddling and cheered enthusiastically at the sight. Moments later they felt the heat and blast of the shock wave on their faces as it shot out across the open water.

Lieutenant Commander Welch brought the landing craft closer to the shore, and an elated group of Marines and UDT men clammered aboard.

To the men on the *Bass*, the explosion was a welcome sight, and when the demolition party returned, an impromptu party was held.

Meanwhile, Major Dupras and Lieutenant Commander Welch had been discussing their next target and had come to the conclusion that they must return to the twin tunnels and bridge they had failed to destroy on the previous night. It was simply too good a target to miss.

The captain of the *Bass*, delighted that his ship had something more "worthwhile" to do—other than escort duty and endlessly patrolling empty seas—headed his ship back to the area it had been in the previous night.

The swimmer scouts saw no lights as they crawled toward the tunnel, so they continued to move closer. As they neared the entrance, they were startled by the sound of voices. They listened intently to the sounds and determined that they were coming from one of the ominous looking pillboxes near the tunnel entrance. They returned to the boat and reported what they had found.

Accompanied by Major Dupras, six Marines and Lieutenant Thomas Fielding led the way to the pillbox. The low sounds of people talking were still coming from the pillbox, and the Marines quietly moved up to it. On a signal from the major, the Marines burst into the pillbox, intent on doing some fast bayonet work. After a few muffled and stifled yells, one of the Marines came out of the pillbox to inform the waiting men that they had discovered a family of four North Korean peasants inside. The family, who had been using the pillbox as a temporary home, was completely surprised by the Marines and had made no attempt to resist. The remaining pillboxes were found to be empty, and the remainder of the Marines and the demolition team were signaled to come ashore.

Fortunately, the fast-moving Marines had not harmed the Korean family. The problem of what to do with them was solved by taking them and their few belongings a safe distance away from the tunnel and by tying the family up. One Marine, left to guard them, was instructed to loosen their bonds when he was given the signal to return to the boats.

It took the demolition team just over an hour to set the charges on the bridge and in the tunnel mouths, and it was nearly 0200 hours when the ring main was connected to nearly two tons of explosives. With the prisoners' bonds loosened, and everyone but the fusepullers and their escorts back at the boats, the detonators were set off.

Ten minutes later a resounding explosion ripped through the night air, and the bridge and tunnel entrances were destroyed.

Admiral Joy was well-pleased with the success of the combined UDT and Marine team and instructed Welch to continue with his raiding.

For the next three days the *Bass* steamed up and down the North Korean coast, stopping every night to put the raiding party ashore to blow up bridges.

On the night of August 17, the *Bass* steamed up the coast to within thirty miles of Ch'ŏngjin, the largest town on the east coast of North Korea. It was much farther north than the ship had ever been, but aerial reconnaissance photographs had revealed a tempting target—two large bridges side by side, one road and one rail, about two hundred yards inland. Welch and the Marine major could not resist the temptation, and the captain of the *Bass* was just as eager as they were.

Using the same strategy as before, the UDT scouts swam ashore ahead of the boats and conducted a reconnaissance mission. They were gone a considerable period of time, and Major Dupras was about to send in some of the Marines to search for them when they were spotted coming across the beach. Their report revealed that they had thoroughly scouted the bridges and the surrounding areas, and could see no sign of any enemy.

The Marines set up defensively, and the demolition team set to work placing the charges. For some reason, the men did not adhere to the rule of silence; perhaps they were overconfident due to their past successes, or because they had heard the scouts' report that there were no enemy soldiers within miles of the target. Whatever the reason, it was a breach of the rules, and Major Dupras repeatedly told the men to be quiet. When the chattering continued, the major decided to use some shock treatment. He climbed up one of the trestles onto the railroad tracks, and in a thundering drill instructor's voice, he roared, "QUIET!"

Marines jumped in fright, and some of the UDT men almost dropped their explosives at the sound of the sudden command. From that moment on, everyone worked in almost complete silence.

Over half the charges had been placed when the major received a surprise. His radio operator informed him that the captain of the *Bass* was calling him. The major quickly grabbed the headset as radio transmissions were only permitted in extreme emergencies. The captain informed him the the ship's lookouts had spotted the dimmed headlights of a vehicle moving along the coast road in the direction of the bridges. Knowing that whatever it was it had to cross the road bridge, he had felt compelled to break the radio silence rule.

Using the ship's sensitive radar to pinpoint its own position, and knowing the exact location of the bridges, the ship's crew could plot the progress of the lights moving toward the raiding party. Almost all the men on the ship were aware of what was going on, and, as a result, they felt as though they were a part of the operation. The crewmen watched the lights as though they were watching a fascinating movie, while the radar operators called the position of the lights every quarter of a mile as they moved along the road.

Major Dupras warned the demolition team of the approaching vehicle and told the men to continue working until he gave the signal, whereupon they were to take cover immediately. He then listened intently to the ship's radar operator call the positions. When the lights were within a quarter of a mile of the bridge, he gave the signal. Everyone took cover underneath the bridges while the major and one of the UDT officers watched from a safe distance.

They held their breath as a truck loaded with enemy soldiers approached the bridge. To their relief, the truck passed over the bridge without even slowing down and continued along the highway. It was not, as they had feared, an enemy patrol coming to check the bridges.

The captain and crew of the *Bass* were also relieved when they saw the lights continue slowly along the road without faltering. They then waited, somewhat impatiently, for their nightly treat of an explosion and the return of their raiding party.

Back on the bridge, with the threat of discovery now safely past, the men continued with their work and finished setting the charges. Shortly afterward, the crew of the *Bass* received its "firework display" and cheered loudly. When the landing craft returned, it was quickly hauled on board the destroyer by an enthusiastic ship's crew.

The *Bass* did not leave the area immediately. Instead, the captain cruised around until daylight and then moved in a little closer to the shore to get a better look at the damaged bridges. The road bridge was totally destroyed, and the main center span of the railroad bridge was in ruins in the river beneath it.

Admiral Joy was well-satisfied with the success of the raiding party, but he now had another job for them. The *Bass* was ordered to steam around to the west coast to conduct reconnaissance work for General MacArthur's planned invasion. This brought to an end a brief but illustrious raiding career for the *Bass* and Lieutenant Commander Welch's Underwater Demolition Team One.

The Marines' and Underwater Demolition Teams' successful raids at the beginning of the Korean War demonstrated to the Navy that the UDT could be used successfully out of the water for limited land operations, either by themselves or with other armed raiders. It was from this success that the initial idea came to train teams from the UDT in more advanced raiding techniques and deep inland penetration and reconnaissance missions—almost the exact role of the modern-day SEALs.

11

BATTLEFIELD LOG:
Rung Sat, Vietnam—1967

Between the sprawling, noisy city of Saigon and the South China Sea lies a river delta and mangrove swamp area that covers some four hundred square miles of the earth's surface.

When viewed from the air, the collage of green could be described as beautiful. However, beneath the undulating canopy of green, the jungle is a dense, tangled mass of sweltering, soggy vegetation, with growing plants and trees fighting for life through the putrifying remains of dead fauna and flora.

Hundreds of rivers and streams feed into the area and then fan out to create the massive delta that stretches to the sea. Most of the area is affected by a four-foot tide that races in and out at speeds from three to four knots; and when the tide is out, the complete area is a mass of stinking, slimy mud that pops and crackles as though it were alive.

The jungle vegetation and the rotting, slimy ground it stands on are both repugnant and almost evil, and, as is the way of nature, creatures that inhabit such territory normally match their surroundings. This region is one of the exceptions to the rule—its inhabitants are infinitely more nasty and more repulsive than their surroundings.

There are alligators that eat anything; toothless pythons that hang from trees like Christmas decorations and have appetites similar to those of "over-toothed" alligators; large red ants whose poisonous bites leave an incredible burning sensation; jungle cats that scream and howl and whose eyes seem to glow in the dark; large rats; blood-sucking leeches; mosquitoes; poisonous snakes and a variety of other reptiles; "lung fish" that live in the slimy mud and gasp and sigh as though they might be human beings; strange-looking birds that attack without warning; and bats that are reputed to suck blood. There are many other creatures and insects, most of which appear to have a perverse sense about them, to the extent that not even the words *mean* and *evil* are adequate to describe them.

Perhaps it is the creatures that are attracted to the environment, and not the environment that develops the character of the creatures. Perhaps it makes no difference; the result would probably still be the same: the Rung Sat—the jungle delta and mangrove swamp between Saigon and the South China Sea.

The area was a veritable nightmare for the average human being—including the fanatical Vietcong, the guerilla soldiers of the North Vietnamese leader Ho Chi Min. However, by early 1966, they had established themselves in the "better areas" of the Rung Sat and were conducting operations against Saigon and the surrounding area, particularly against the extensive river traffic that transported South Vietnam's vital food supplies.

Early in 1966, SEAL Team One was in operation in what was officially termed the "Rung Sat Special Zone." This Vietcong lair required special attention, and, as none of the Regular South Vietnamese Army units would go anywhere near the area, the SEALs were given the job.

At first the SEALs spent months conducting reconnaissance patrols in the worst possible areas of the zone, namely those regions surrounding the better areas that the Vietcong were using as base camps and supply dumps.

When the months of incredible reconnaissance work were completed, with the SEALs often sitting for hours within fifty feet of the enemy, it was decided that the time had come to let the enemy know that there were other creatures in the abysmal jungle—other than its natural inhabitants—that they should be afraid of.

A unit called Detachment Golf of SEAL Team One operated almost exclusively in the Rung Sat. During the later stages of the conflict in Vietnam, captured enemy documents revealed that not only were the Vietcong afraid to go where the SEALs went, but they were terrified of the "wild animals" of Detachment Golf. This fact had previously been stated by some Hoi Chanh (Vietcong defectors), and it had confirmed what the SEALs had hoped for—that they would be the terrorists of the Rung Sat, not the Vietcong.

One team from Detachment Golf had been given information that a pagoda in the middle of the jungle was being used to store weapons, and the men set out to destroy it. Using one of their specialized boats, a heavily armed small platoon of twelve men, led by a lieutenant and a chief petty officer, navigated their way up the river toward a landing point that was near the pagoda.

As they rounded a bend in the river, close to where they were intending to land, they spotted six men wearing the type of black pajamas that were the favored uniform of the Vietcong. The men were armed with rifles, and, on seeing the SEAL boat, they started running toward a small hut a little way from the water's edge.

The experienced SEALs (the average age of the men in this platoon was twenty-eight), who were not known for wasting ammunition by shooting at the enemy when they were not at close range, held their fire and waited for their lieutenant to call the action. As he ordered the boat to head for the bank, the Vietcong started shooting from inside the hut. The lieutenant turned to a seaman carrying a 57-mm recoilless rifle and casually requested that the man put a round in the roof of the hut. The seaman nodded, sighted the weapon from the moving boat, and squeezed the firing handle. The weapon responded with a deep cracking sound, and a "soft target" high explosive round embedded itself in the roof and exploded.

When the enemy continued to fire, the lieutenant called for a round in the window. Another crack from the 57 and a round whistled in through the window. With a shrug of his shoulders the lieutenant called for a shot in the door, and the gunner simply complied—it was his day to be on target. Another round through the now empty door caused the building to explode. The enemy fire stopped.

As the SEALs scrambled ashore, they saw a large group of the enemy appear a little farther along the river bank, and a tremendous firefight ensued. The first six men they had shot were the rearguard of a battalion of Vietcong who were on their way to collect arms from the pagoda.

The SEALs, despite the fact that they were heavily outnumbered, steadily advanced through the jungle toward the enemy and continued to pick them off. After about half an hour, the lieutenant called off the chase—to pursue the enemy any further would just increase the possibility of his platoon being ambushed.

Returning to the boat, they collected spare ammunition and set out through the jungle toward the pagoda.

After about three hours of working their way quietly through the dense jungle, the scout signaled the men to halt. Everyone watched the scout's hand signals, a system of communication devised by the SEALs to eliminate the necessity for talking. He had located a group of about twenty of the enemy coming toward the platoon; they were carrying arms and ammunition and had obviously come from the pagoda. The SEALs quickly set up an ambush line and waited patiently.

Fifteen minutes later they heard the quick chatter of the approaching Vietcong, and their hands tightened on their weapons. As the leading enemy came into view, the 57-mm rifle opened the ambush, with the first round instantly killing the leading pair of Vietcong. Four more of the enemy died within seconds from a hail of fire put up by the rest of the platoon, and the remainder of the enemy dropped their loads and dispersed into the jungle.

As a result of the ambush, the lieutenant decided that to continue toward the pagoda would not be a good idea. The enemy at the pagoda would definitely have heard the ambush and would either be waiting for them or preparing patrols to search for them.

He had the chief petty officer take an accurate compass reading, something which he could not trust himself to do as he had numerous pieces of shrapnel from previous missions still embedded in his body, and they could seriously affect the sensitive navigation compass. There were others in the platoon who had the same problem; their colleagues just would not trust them to take compass readings.

He kept the platoon heading south into one of the worst areas of the mangrove swamps; the chances were that even if the enemy troops located their trail, they would not follow them into the festering swamp.

They were wading through a fetid, swamp channel just before dark when a gunner's mate became temporarily stuck in the soggy bottom below. As he quietly started to work his legs free, he saw an old log floating in his direction;

but experience told him that it was not a log. He quietly and quickly signaled to his nearest colleague. The trapped gunner's mate removed the magazine from his M-16 and silently ejected the round from the chamber of the barrel. The seaman he had signaled was quickly wading toward him and had followed his example. When the alligator had drifted within three feet of him, the gunner's mate hit it squarely between the eyes with the butt of the M-16. As the great gnarled beast swung his head upward and to one side, the butt of the seaman's weapon caught him on top of his right eye. With a great flurry of thrashing and continuing blows from the two SEALs, the surprised beast withdrew. The gunner's mate nodded his thanks and was about to ask for assistance to get his legs unstuck when he suddenly realized he was free. As the two men waded to the bank, they saw the remainder of the platoon standing there quietly laughing.

Shortly afterward the scout found a clump of mangroves that were above the muddy waters, and the lieutenant signaled that they would use it as a harbor for the night.

Sentries were posted as the remainder of the platoon found places to settle down, all close to one another. For the next few hours, they listened intently to the strange sounds of the jungle swamp. They were sounds that this group of SEALs was very familiar with, but the SEALs could take no chances with the cunning enemy. There was just a possibility that the enemy would follow.

When the jungle settled into its nighttime noises, so did those SEALs who were not on sentry duty. There was no eating, talking, or smoking. Most of the men ate little or nothing while they were on patrol in the Rung Sat, although they all carried food in the form of special Emergency Ration Packs.

Before dawn the team was on the move again, slowly working its way back through the swamps in the direction of the pagoda.

By 1000 hours the men had silently crept within fifty feet of the building, but could see no movement. They remained in their positions without moving for the next three hours; they just watched and listened for anything that would indicate they were walking into a trap. The chief petty officer half lay, half crouched, alongside a large tree, and he had a good view of the pagoda; the lieutenant was about fifteen feet away to his left, and he, too, was watching the building and its approaches. About fifteen feet behind them were a gunner's mate and a boatswain's mate; both were in a position to watch the rear and part of the flanks.

They had been waiting for about twenty minutes, and their ears were well accustomed to the sounds around them, when a strange noise was heard. The chief petty officer heard it first and could not quite determine where it was coming from. It was not the sound of a human; he could easily distinguish any human movement from that of an animal. As he looked at the boatswain's mate, he noticed that the man's eyes were looking above his head, and he was signaling the chief not to move. The boatswain's mate was slowly pulling out the razor-sharp knife that the chief had seen him use like a surgeon on numerous occasions. He also knew that the man could throw the knife more accurately than most men could shoot, so whatever it was that was above him would probably get a surprise.

The chief found out what it was a few moments later when a huge form came into view a few feet from his head. It was the body of a massive python, and it slid slowly down onto the ground beside the chief. The SEALs who saw the creature, including the lieutenant, swore it was at least thirty feet long. The chief just said it was big. The monster python, however, did not move when it landed on the ground beside the chief; it sat there with its head not two feet from his face and just stared at him.

For the next two and a half hours, the staring contest continued. The chief swore he blinked normally; the others swore he didn't blink the entire period. Finally, the massive reptile decide to end the contest and slowly moved away, passing very close to the horrified gunner's mate. The chief later stated that pythons had quite pretty faces. No one argued; they now considered him an expert in the subject.

When the python had left, the lieutenant signaled the platoon to move toward the pagoda. A careful search showed that the place was empty and well booby trapped. The SEALs added a few booby traps of their own before leaving and heading back toward the river where they had first encountered the enemy.

They were almost half way to the river when their scout was seen moving quickly back toward them. He explained that a group of Vietcong—approximately fifty strong—were strung out in an ambush line ahead and were well concealed. The lieutenant and the chief worked out a counter ambush plan that would require the SEALs to take the enemy by surprise on the west or right flank.

After an hour of very careful maneuvering, they came up behind about fifteen of the enemy huddled in a tight group over two machine guns; four Vietcong manned the guns, and the remainder were armed with automatic weapons. One of the SEALs, a semiprofessional baseball player before he entered the Navy, moved a little farther to the rear and quietly hurled a grenade far to the front and toward the east flank of the ambush line.

The sound of the falling grenade caused a burst of fire from the east flank, and when it exploded, the SEALs opened up from behind the enemy machine gunners.

In the fierce firefight that followed, eleven of the enemy were killed and the remainder fled, except one, who had been knocked unconscious by the butt of an M-16 that had driven off the alligator. The man was now bound and gagged, and thrown over the shoulder of one of the gunner's mates as the SEALs quickly left the area.

It was now too dangerous to remain in the area. The enemy troops had been surprised too many times and had taken a beating—they would start searching in force very shortly. The lieutenant broke his radio silence and called for an exfiltration by helicopter. He gave his status as "a SEAL platoon plus one bundle," a signal to the intelligence officers that he had a Vietcong prisoner.

About an hour later, a giant CH47 helicopter escorted by six Huey gunships arrived at the exfiltration point, and the SEALs with their now conscious, but bewildered, bundle were quickly lifted out.

One of the SEALs who had never had a nickname in his entire life now had one—he was forevermore known as The Python.

12

SEAL TEAM—PAST AND PRESENT

The Underwater Demolition Teams were the first SEAL Teams, and as far back as World War II, they were performing missions that were identical in size and scope to those of the present-day SEALs.

When the Underwater Demolition Teams were first put into operation, they were classified as a top-secret unit—the chiefs of staff obviously did not want the enemy knowing exactly how we gathered our information concerning their beach defenses, nor how we removed those defenses. If the enemy had been privy to the full details of the teams' methods of operation, it would have effected suitable counter measures, which would simply have prolonged the war and cost the lives of many more men.

At the end of the war, the strict secrecy requirement was lifted when most of the teams were disbanded, but the advent of the Korean War again produced a need for secrecy. By this time, almost every military organization in the world knew the operating methods and procedures of the Underwater Demolition Team, and it did not seem to have much effect on the outcome of the war.

However, the United States Navy realized that it could not continue to develop new tactics, equipment, methods, and techniques, and make them generally known to the world. It was pointless, as any or all of the new developments would be useless when another conflict started, simply because the enemy would already have developed the appropriate countermeasures.

However, some principles do not change much, particularly those that have been properly thought out and well developed. This was certainly the case with the Underwater Demolition Team and the majority of their methods of training and operating, because the majority of those methods are still in use to this day.

After the Korean War, the Navy came to the conclusion that, although there was nothing that could be done concerning the information that was already publicly known about the elite Underwater Demolition Teams, there was something that could be done about all further developments: they could be classified as secret again.

It was to be discovered, within a very short period of time, that once any elite group that employs secret tactics is made highly visible, it becomes almost impossible to bring a tight security system back into operation.

It was just such a situation that faced the Navy concerning the Underwater Demolition Teams in the late fifties.

Apart from the fact that the physical requirements for entry into the team were more demanding than in any other branch of the armed forces, some of the UDT developments in tactics and equipment were showing signs of being extremely useful in another type of warfare—namely in operations behind enemy lines. It was a job that had been done, to an extent, by the OSS during World War II; but the OSS had long since been disbanded, and its re-formation was out of the question.

The Underwater Demolition Team offered the best possibility of developing a new group within its existing structure to suit the Navy's requirements, and orders were issued for the formation of the group.

In 1958, the first Sea, Air, and Land Unit was formed within the Underwater Demolition Team; and when the men were cross-trained in the disciplines of the other services, it was realized that the small unit was extremely useful, much more so than had originally been thought. As a result, it was decided that it would be useful to have a few more of these highly trained men available, and several more units were organized.

However, the problem of security again raised its head, as word was leaking out that the Underwater Demolition Teams were changing their role. At that time it was not true—a handful of men had simply been specially trained in order to allow the Underwater Demolition Team to be able to respond to unusual requests for "extra" effort during the conduct of their traditional duties.

The problem was solved, in a manner of speaking, by President Kennedy in the latter part of 1961. It was his belief that the United States should have available a military organization that could engage in the type of warfare that the Soviets were subjecting us to. He knew of the Underwater Demolition Teams and of their Hell Week training; and when he discovered that they had a small, specialized group called the Sea, Air, and Land Unit, he realized that he had found the basis of the new organization.

Once again, the foresight of the men of the Underwater Demolition Teams showed its value in a time of need. President Kennedy directed that these Sea, Air, and Land Units of the Underwater Demolition Team should be separated from the main organization, put under a strict security blanket, and renamed SEAL Team One and SEAL Team Two. The president also directed that the SEALs be further trained in other specialized disciplines and that all new members meet the high entry requirement standards that were already in existence. That last statement was taken to mean that all new members must go through the Underwater Demolition Team training school.

With the assignment of its security-sensitive offspring to its own command, the Underwater Demolition Team continued pioneering and developing new techniques for demolition and reconnaissance; all newly developed methods and technology were, of course, shared with the SEAL Team.

Prior to the Vietnam conflict, the newly commissioned SEALs saw service during the Cuban crisis in 1962, and in the Dominican Republic in 1965; and it was during this period that they also developed their own special tactics and methods of operation.

With the advent of the Vietnam War, the SEALs went into action alongside the Underwater Demolition Teams. However, nothing was known about SEAL operations until word was leaked out, in the form of a cartoon about a SEAL team that had landed in North Vietnam and had reputedly stolen a complete Soviet surface-to-air missile. The SEALs were, of course, extremely alarmed by this, and security was tightened even further; but the cat was out of the bag as far as operations in Vietnam were concerned, and the news-hungry media were given a limited amount of information.

Records show that during the Vietnam conflict, there were no more than two hundred SEALs and that, in their first year of operation, they conducted 153 missions and only had one man killed in action. By the end of the war, the SEAL Team had accounted for 580 Vietcong killed, confirmed by body count, a probable 300 more killed, and in excess of a thousand taken prisoner.

During the conflict, the SEAL Team became perhaps the most decorated unit of its size, earning two Presidential Unit Citations, one Navy Unit Commendation, and one Meritorious Unit Commendation.

Individual awards for valor were one Medal of Honor, two Navy Crosses, forty-two Silver Stars, 402 Bronze Stars, two Legions of Merit, 352 Navy Commendation Medals, and fifty-one Navy Achievement Medals.

With the end of the Vietnam War, security was further tightened, but it is openly admitted that SEALs have been involved in exercises with both our own forces and our NATO Allies throughout the world.

More recently, it is known that the SEALs played a vital part, in conjunction with the U. S. Rangers and the Marines, in the taking of the island of Grenada.

In October 1983, the Underwater Demolition Team and the SEALs finally came back together under the new name: the SEALs.

Because the Underwater Demolition Team's mission role was so close to that of the SEALs' in basic concept—because all SEALs were trained by the Underwater Demolition Team, and because in this modern age, the methods, tactics, and equipment of the Underwater Demolition Team have become so sophisticated and vital to the nation's security—it had been decided that the strategies had to be made more secure from our enemies. The obvious way for the Navy to go about this was to enlarge the SEALs and, at the same time, further protect some of the nation's vital defense secrets.

Information concerning the present-day SEALs is not available—and that, in itself, is a secret weapon.

ABOUT THE AUTHOR

IAN PADDEN was born and educated in England. During service with the British Military he learned to fly and also developed an interest in specialized reconnaissance, espionage, and counter insurgency warfare. His interests in these subjects required him to have a thorough knowledge of other special ("elite") military units throughout the world.

He was taught deep-sea diving by Royal Navy instructors and worked as a commercial diver in construction, salvage, and offshore oil drilling. He spent further time in the oil industry working as a driller, drilling supervisior and drilling engineer and was later employed by one of the world's leading subsea drilling equipment manufacturers as a specialist engineer and training instructor. He left the company to become a drilling consultant, and in that capacity has been responsible for drilling oil wells, both on land and offshore, throughout the world.

One of Ian's hobbies is aerobatic competition flying. He has been a member of the British Aerobatic Team since 1978 and has represented Great Britain in two world championships.

Ian Padden began writing in 1963 when he presented a special paper on "The Foundation, Formation and Operating Principles of the Roman Army" to the British Army School of Education. In 1965 he assisted in the writing of "The Principles of Diving" by Mark Terrell (Stanley Paul; London). During his career in the oil industry, he was commissioned to write training manuals and narrations for training films. He had also written two television scripts and various treatments for documentaries. He is currently finishing a full-length novel.

The Fighting Elite ™

AMERICA'S GREAT MILITARY UNITS

by Ian Padden

Here is the magnificent new series that brings you into the world of America's most courageous and spectacular combat forces—the Fighting Elite. Each book is an exciting account of a particular military unit—its origins and training programs, its weaponry and deployment—and lets you re-live its most famous battles in tales of war and valor that will live forever. All the books include a special 8-page photo insert.